Seeds
of
Discovery

Seeds
of
Discovery

a sequel to
The Art of Scientific Investigation

W. I. B. Beveridge

Emeritus Professor of Animal Pathology
University of Cambridge

W·W·NORTON & COMPANY
New York · London

Library of Congress Cataloging in Publication Data

Beveridge, William Ian Beardmore, 1980–
  Seeds of discovery.
  Bibliography: p.
  Includes index.
  1. Research—Methodology. I. Title.
Q180.55.M4B48   507'.2   80–22863
ISBN 0–393–01444–4

W. W. Norton & Company, Inc. 500 Fifth Avenue, New York, N.Y. 10110
W. W. Norton & Company Ltd. 25 New Street Square, London EC4A 3NT

1 2 3 4 5 6 7 8 9 0

Contents

List of illustrations

Preface

This book is about scientific discovery, that is, the non-technical aspects of research, the mental procedures that lead to discoveries. It is a sequel to the book I wrote some thirty years ago on the same theme — *The Art of Scientific Investigation*. Most of the ideas expounded then have stood up well to the critics and the test of time, and hardly any need revision; but some of the subjects can now be developed further and there are some fresh topics that need to be considered. The two fields in which the most important advances have been made are the psychology of creativity and systems theory. The study of creativity has progressed to a remarkable degree over the last twenty years, but so far its applications have been mainly in education and in industry; scientists are mostly unaware of the vast literature that has grown up on the subject. The systems theory has revolutionized thinking in many aspects of science and technology but its implications are not yet realized in some disciplines.

Like my earlier work, the book is addressed primarily at the young scientist, but I hope that some more senior scientists and general readers may also find it of interest. It is written in language that anyone with a general education can understand easily; it is not intended for the specialists in the fields reviewed. Practising scientists are mostly too occupied with their own work to give time to studying the diffuse literature on the psychology of inventive thinking and on the philosophy of science. Nor is it only a matter of available time; many of the writers on these subjects use concepts and terms unfamiliar to the scientist. Yet clearly these matters lie at the very heart of research and scientists should have some knowledge of them. I have endeavoured to present a concise review of those aspects of most interest to the scientist and key references are provided for those who wish to read further. It will be obvious to the reader that I have no specialist knowledge of some of the subjects touched on, and that to some extent the book is a statement of my personal views.

So far as possible I have avoided repeating what is already expounded in *The Art of Scientific Investigation*. Consequently this book presents an incomplete picture of research. For a comprehensive analysis of the various facets of a scientist's work, both books should be read.

Many women, I hope, will be included among my readers. I ask them to forgive me for referring to the scientist always as masculine. This does not reflect a bias against women scientists, it is merely to avoid innumerable repetitions of 'men and women', 'his or her' and other such cumbersome phrases.

I wish to thank warmly several colleagues who kindly read the typescript and offered helpful criticism, in particular Mohammed Abdussalam, Norman Bailey, Alan Betts, John Beveridge, Konrad Bögel, Jean-Paul Dustin, John Hearn, Martin Kaplan and Calvin Schwabe. Also I am much indebted to Miss Margaret McKean for careful typing, for great patience with innumerable alterations, and for help with indexing and proof-reading.

1980 W. I. B. Beveridge
Canberra

Acknowledgements

For their kind permission to reproduce photographs in this book, the Author wishes to thank the following:

Lotte Meitner-Graf, for Sir Karl Popper
Popperfoto, for Jacques Monod
The World Health Organization, for Sir Hans Krebs, Albert Sabin
The Children's Medical Research Foundation (Australia), for Sir Norman Gregg
Arthur Koestler
Edward de Bono
Sir Peter Medawar
Sir John Eccles
Robert Good
James Watson
John Cade

The cartoon in Chapter 2 is reproduced with the permission of Hoff, and *The New Yorker Magazine*, Inc.

Seeds
of
Discovery

I

Producing ideas and solving problems

'Novelties come from previously unseen association of old
material. To create is to re-combine.'
FRANÇOIS JACOB

THE CREATIVE PROCESS

'The Creative Process in Science and Medicine' was the subject
of a symposium at Kronberg, Germany, in which twenty-four
eminent scientists, including four Nobel Prizewinners, took
part in 1974.[63] Opening the discussion, Sir Karl Popper,
probably the leading authority in the world today on the
philosophy of science, remarked that the subject is vast, and
also dangerous because so much nonsense has been written
about it. The literature on creativity has become formidably
large: over the last twenty years thousands of articles and
books on it have been published. Much is repetitive and much
superficial. In this chapter I shall endeavour to summarize
those aspects of the subject most relevant to research and useful
to the scientist, and to avoid the ill-founded speculations and
trivialities that Popper warned against.

At the outset let us be quite clear about the subject we are
dealing with in this chapter, for creativity is a much abused
word today. We are considering the process of generating new
ideas in science—new concepts and theories—inventive thinking applied to the solution of practical and theoretical problems,
and the advancement of knowledge and understanding thereby.
Creation in this sense consists of perceiving new significant
patterns in bits of knowledge—data and theories—already
available, just as a musical composer creates a new melody by
devising a fresh arrangement of musical notes. By combining,

relating and integrating previously separate pieces of information a new thought-pattern, i.e. idea, is created. Even material creations usually start in this way. The basic process of innovative thinking is the same in science, the arts, business, or any occupation that is not purely routine or just following instructions. Psychologists call it intuition, philosophers call it induction. The essence of innovation is that the way to it is not known beforehand; therefore it is impossible to predict it logically.

It is not necessary to be a mechanic in order to drive a car, nor trained in cognitive psychology (study of the thinking process) or philosophy in order to think or reason. But there are times when the car will not go and times when the usual thought processes do not solve a problem and then it is useful to have a working knowledge of the machinery one is using. This knowledge need not be profound; it often helps to get the car going again if one just knows the general principles of how the machine functions and some techniques that are useful in overcoming common difficulties.

In his book *The Act of Creation*, Arthur Koestler developed the thesis that most new ideas are discovered by perceiving the relationship or analogy between two quite different fields of activity, what he called 'matrices'.[58] A 'matrix' is a scientific discipline, profession, craft, skill, or any activity governed by a recognized pattern of behaviour or thought. When one succeeds in seeing the connection or analogy between two matrices the result may be a new idea or a joke. Many writers have pointed out that a sudden flash of illumination in science is similar to cracking a joke in that you suddenly switch from one way of looking at the subject to another—you see points of resemblance between two apparently unrelated subjects, a mating of incompatibles. Like the joke, the bright idea is often greeted with laughter. A nimble wit, a lively mind, perceives connections between different matrices that may lead to a humorous juxtaposition or a scientific insight. There is a striking analogy here with conception in the biological sense, the bringing together of two gametes in fertilization to create a new individual. The interface between two scientific disciplines is often a fertile field to cultivate; for example molecular biology was the offspring of the marriage of chemistry and biology.

It is generally appreciated that major advances in science are usually the consequences of new theories, technical procedures or apparatuses. It is not so well understood that often the starting point of a new theory, the initial spark, is a new concept. By concept I mean an idea around which a theory is built, but which is not itself the theory. A theory commonly concerns the relationship between two or more things, often one of cause and effect. A concept is the kernel of the theory, the thing itself; for instance, atom, electron, gene. The concept often derives from a metaphor or analogy, which can be important aids to thought, as for example the adoption by science of the concept of program as developed in computer technology. Professor J. Z. Young has pointed out what a far-reaching effect this idea has had in biology, especially molecular biology, embryology, and the study of behaviour.[101] One well-developed field in which the principle of analogy has been successfully used is the study of models in comparative medicine. To facilitate research into the underlying mechanisms of a human disease, an analogous disease in animals is sought to serve as a model—either one occurring naturally or one produced artificially. The disease is investigated in the model and the knowledge so gained is applied to the human disease.[9]

A striking exposition of the power of metaphor to stimulate insight was given by the poet William Blake:

> To see a world in a grain of sand,
> And a heaven in a wild flower;
> Hold infinity in the palm of your hand,
> And eternity in an hour.

WAYS OF THINKING

A number of different ways of thinking have been described by psychologists, but for the purpose of the present discussion I propose the following simple classification.

(a) *Critical thinking* is disciplined and largely directed by one's consciousness. It follows logical pathways and stops lines of thought that are inconsistent with known facts and accepted theories. At each step one asks: is this true, is it well established, are there alternatives? This type of thinking is characteristic of the trained mind. During all his education the scientist is trained to think and work logically and systematically.

(b) *Imaginative thinking* is free flowing, not usually consciously directed, and often subjective. It is used especially by children but also by educated adults, for instance when day-dreaming. Imaginative thinking is largely a matter of what the psychologists call 'associative flow'—letting one's train of thought wander and follow associations, relationships, linking one thing to another—similarities, analogies, thought connections of any sort. Dreams during sleep often conjure up ludicrous situations; one can do much the same during 'day-dreaming'. Creating mental images can be done deliberately—picturing in one's mind the components and structure of the problem. Words are the material of critical thinking, but they can be a hindrance in inventive thinking. Many great scientists, Einstein among them, have used visual symbols instead of verbal symbols when trying to solve a problem.[52] Some scientists imagine themselves being one of the elements of the problem, such as a particle in an atomic nucleus or a cell in the body fighting invading microbes. As well as letting thoughts flow freely, one can deliberately look for associations and analogies—direct one's thinking along certain lines not previously explored.

(c) *Wild thinking* is even less disciplined than imaginative thinking. Unaided imagination has its own ingrained inhibitions, conditioned lines of thought, bias. To escape from these, techniques that aid wild thinking have been devised and are the basis of brainstorming, lateral thinking, and the morphological approach. They are designed to break up established habits of thought-associations and to probe new ways of looking at the subject. Seemingly irrelevant information and wild ideas are entertained in an effort to disturb ways of thinking and to direct thoughts along new channels. It has long been known that breaking out from conventional thinking is a major factor in creative thinking, and this was reaffirmed at the Kronberg symposium. Many scientists, philosophers, and psychologists have emphasized that the mental act of invention, of intuition, is a non-rational activity. The advocates of wild thinking believe it can best be sought by deliberately invoking a chaotic, irrational mood in which bizarre analogies that are normally censored by the subconscious are brought into the conscious mind. Far-fetched analogies help one to get around barriers erected by previous unsuccessful attempts. Often you do not know what you are looking for till you have found it, so you cannot see in advance the right track to it; the only way is to cast around at random, relying on your ability to recognize it when you happen upon it.

Each type of thinking has its advantages and its limitations; each is useful in the appropriate place. The usual procedure in research is to follow critical thinking and only when that fails to switch to imaginative thinking to try to find a way around the difficulty. If that also fails to show a way ahead one may resort to wild thinking in the hope of seeing the problem in a new light. Then if some promising idea comes up one reverts to critical thinking to work it out. In practice the different ways of thinking are not sharply separated activities; one jumps back and forth from one to the other continuously.

One must not lose sight of the fact that disciplined, critical thinking is the basic *modus operandi* of science—one could say it is an essential characteristic not only of science but of all scholarly endeavours. Having made this point quite firmly, I can now say that it is not the whole of science and not the most appropriate thinking for discovering new concepts, theories, and techniques, so in this chapter we are concerned more with the other forms of thought and with the artistic aspects of science. Sir Karl Popper put it well: 'Bold ideas, unjustifiable anticipations, and speculative thought, are our only means for interpreting nature: our only organon, our only instrument, for grasping her'.[82]

PRESCRIPTION FOR GENERATING INTUITIONS

The procedure described here has been reported by many scientists and other thinkers as well as by psychologists as the principal mental technique whereby new concepts are invented. The procedure is by no means new, but it is still the most commonly used by an individual working alone. And most important discoveries still originate in one person's mind, even if he is a member of a team. The tremendous volume of research that has been done in creative thinking over the last twenty years has not rendered this technique out of date, but rather confirmed it and shown that it is a skill that can be cultivated.

For convenience of exposition, the technique can be broken down into four stages, although in practice the stages may not be separated and they often overlap. They are (1) Collection of information, (2) Contemplation, (3) Conception, and (4) Criticism of the new idea—the four Cs of Creativity. If during the last stage the idea is rejected, as it is in the majority of cases, one reverts to stage 2 or even right back to stage 1.

1. *Collection of information*

Information considered to be relevant, or possibly relevant, to the problem is collected by searching the scientific literature, by observation and experiment, and from various other sources such as hospital records, surveys, enquiries, and discussion with colleagues or anyone concerned even remotely with the problem. At the Kronberg symposium the point was made that it is especially valuable to collect information and opinions that appear to be in conflict with one another, or that challenge prevailing beliefs. Interaction and friction are conducive to creativity. Oddities are often the starting point of a new line of investigation. Close personal contact with the problem often leads to observation of details that otherwise would be missed, also it stimulates the imagination. It may give a subconscious feeling of familiarity with the subject, an understanding that cannot be recorded in objective terms.

The information is assembled systematically. The problem is clearly defined and perhaps broken down into sub-problems. The objectives of the investigation are set out in general terms. At this stage it is important to identify carefully the scientific questions that one is going to try to answer; this determines what direction the investigation takes. The problem is some- times solved during this stage without any radically new ideas being invoked, but if the problem is a difficult one it will have to be carried to the next stage.

2. *Contemplation*

The marshalled information is carefully scrutinized from every possible point of view. It is assimilated and digested. Francis Bacon said one should first prepare the mind by clearing it of all preconcieved notions and prejudices; in present day language we would say one should keep an open mind. Each point is examined minutely in relation to the other bits of information, looking for significant associations. The reasons behind the facts are pondered: why is this or that the way it is? What causes it? Are there analogies with situations outside this problem? Various aspects of the problem are visualised in the mind. One's thoughts tend to follow the same path each time; to break away from this rut, it helps to start again from a different aspect of the problem. Another tactic is to imagine the problem solved and turn it around and try to work backwards. An effort should be made to be bold and unconventional, even if it requires courage to do so. Accepted views enshrined in the literature should be questioned. One needs to have a strong desire for a solution, a feeling of being personally involved, and optimistic. Francis Bacon said: 'They are ill discoverers that think there is no land, when they can see nothing but sea'. Creative thinking requires real application and a positive attitude.

Discuss the problem with a colleague or anyone willing to talk about it with you. Sir Hans Krebs and many other successful scientists have testified that discussion is a powerful aid to innovative thinking. Dr James Watson's book *The Double Helix* is an outstanding illustration of the value of exchange and interplay of ideas with a colleague.[96] Discussion with a non-scientist can also be useful. Lord Rutherford said one should be able to explain any problem to a barmaid.[50] Niels Bohr is said to have needed the stimulus of discussion to start his thinking.[86] Dialogue provokes the mind to get away from thinking along the same groove, the same memory trace.

Solutions, or possible solutions, to easy problems are soon found, but difficult problems have to be puzzled over persistently for days, weeks or even months. The mind becomes saturated with all the relevant information and one reaches the stage when 'you cannot get it off your mind', and whatever one is doing it keeps popping back into one's thoughts, even perhaps into one's dreams. This is a common experience. To give just one example, Dr James Watson said in his book 'even during good films I found it almost impossible to forget bases'. When this state of near-obsession is reached, one has the 'prepared mind' and is ready for the next stage.

3. *Conception*

The sudden insight, the flash of illumination in which a possible solution appears, may come at any time, sometimes when one is puzzling over the problem, but more often when one has temporarily abandoned it and is occupied with some undemanding, relaxing activity—having a bath, lying in bed (especially in the morning), walking in the country, listening to a concert, or watching a cinema film or television. Sometimes there comes a point when the mind is stale, having been over the same ground time and time again so that thoughts are in a rut. Then it is best to stop deliberately puzzling over it for a few days, take a holiday or become occupied with some diversion or hobby, but not one that requires mental concentration. The remarkable thing about intuitions is that you do not arrive at them by a train of conscious thought; they seem to come spontaneously. Apparently they are worked out in the subconscious mind. They bring excitement and pleasure. One has the feeling of seeing something no one has ever seen before and there is an instinctive urge to tell somebody about it. However, the bright idea does not always come in a blinding flash. Sometimes there are preliminary, precursory hints that lead up to it. Just as one sometimes dimly glimpses things at the periphery of one's field of vision, one sometimes has a feeling that there is a vague idea lurking at the edge of one's consciousness. The sensation may be similar to the irritation one experiences when having difficulty in recalling someone's name, or it may be pleasurable in anticipation of enlightenment. As John Masefield said:

> ... when you find
> No highway more, no track, all being blind,
> The way to go shall glimmer in the mind.

Occasionally the intuition is sparked off by some chance observation, a point that has been neglected by most writers on the subject. The classical example is the Archimedes story, which is recounted in the Appendix. While lying in his bath, he suddenly realized that the amount of water his body displaced was equal to the volume of that part of his body that was immersed; this gave him the clue as to how he could measure the volume of the king's crown and from that work out whether it was made of pure gold. His exclamation *'eureka!'* (I have found it) has echoed down the centuries.

In problem-oriented research the new realization may be the practical solution being sought for the particular problem; in pure research it may be a synthesis linking together many ideas and pieces of information into a new generalization in which the whole is greater than the sum of the parts; that is, a new principle may be discerned—the height of creativity in science.

4. *Criticism*

The new idea must then be examined critically to see if it is consistent with the facts of the situation and current theories. Sad to say, more often than not the brain child is found not to be viable. But even when there is some contrary evidence, the new thought should not be hastily discarded. Sometimes it can be modified to fit the facts, or it may lead on to a further profitable line of thought, a fresh approach to the problem. Occasionally the 'facts' may be shown to be wrong. But it is not sensible to become so attached to one's little creation that one sticks to it in the face of irrefutable contrary arguments. Fortunately the fruitful mind will throw up many intuitions and it is better to look for other ideas than to adhere to a hopeless one. Nor should one possible solution exclude another; the most successful thinkers often entertain simultaneously a number of alternative hypotheses to be checked. Many distinguished scientists have said that ideas come to them frequently but the great majority are quickly seen to be wrong and rejected. There is an old Chinese proverb that the best way to catch fish is to have many lines.

LATERAL THINKING

Dr Edward de Bono of Cambridge introduced the term lateral thinking as the name for certain mental procedures of inventive thinking based on theories which he has expounded in a series of publications over the last twelve years.[23.24] His books are aimed mainly at industrialists and school children. Curiously, neither he, nor anyone else so far as I know, has yet advocated applying lateral thinking to scientific research, where I believe it has much to offer. It is somewhat similar to wild thinking and de Bono has developed ways of cultivating it. I hope the brief outline that follows will encourage scientists to use it.

De Bono regards the brain as a mechanical system that processes information presented to it in certain ways which he describes with the aid of simple analogies. It is a self-organizing system that necessarily forms patterns which become in-grained. Memory may be likened to the surface of a jelly on which is poured hot water that forms channels and pools. These affect the behaviour of any subsequent water put on it. Patterns are formed that become more and more set with use and then only a clue is needed to start thoughts automatically running the same course. These deeply in-built habits are difficult to escape from, but there are certain techniques that help to do so.

Vertical thinking is the name de Bono gives to the ordinary way of thinking in science and everyday life. It is straight ahead, orthodox thinking in which one step follows another rationally, the chain of thoughts flowing along the lines of greatest probability. This is the natural way the mind works most of the time, especially trained minds, and it is the most effective in the majority of situations. As de Bono defines vertical thinking it is not quite the same as critical thinking in my classification, but it is similar in most respects.

Lateral thinking is quite different. It resembles what I have described as wild thinking, and each step has a low probability of being correct. De Bono has developed ways of using it as a tool for attaining new insights. It is a technique that enables the mind to escape from established patterns and habits of thought. It fosters variety and seeks as many alternative approaches as possible. Whereas vertical thinking selects the most probable and excludes the others, lateral thinking does not try to be correct at every step. Unlikely paths are explored in the hope of finding unforeseen new concepts which are then examined by vertical thinking. Lateral thinking can be likened to firing a shot gun at a bush in which you think there are some birds though you cannot see them.

De Bono says conflict is the only way to change ideas. Therefore lateral thinking is deliberately provocative in order to confront and disturb the existing way of looking at a subject. One's memory and conventional habits of thought have a fierce selective effect in directing one's line of thought and must be restrained if one is to overcome barriers and break through to new light.

So much then for the nature and purpose of lateral thinking. De Bono has described procedures for using this way of thinking in his book *Lateral Thinking: A Textbook of Creativity*. So as to be brief and at the same time explicit, I have abstracted his presentation to a series of precepts that summarize the essentials of his method.

The first precept is to cultivate a habit of looking for as many different approaches to a problem as possible, rather than sticking to what appears to be the most promising way of tackling the problem. One may set oneself a quota of alternatives; this acts as a stimulus to keep hunting around in the mind for other ways of looking at the problem, for analogies and possible connections. Nearly always alternatives can be found if one looks hard enough for them.

The second precept is to challenge assumptions. Generally in thinking about something one makes several assumptions—often they seem so obvious that they are unconsciously taken for granted. But when scrutinized sceptically they may prove dubious or unjustified and thus thought-barriers are removed.

The third precept is to suspend judgement of the ideas that spring into the mind. It is well known that many discoveries have come from following false trails. Therefore do not dismiss an idea without first exploring where it might lead to; it may breed further ideas. The aim is to happen upon a new significant thought combination without regard to the route there.

The fourth precept is to visualize the problem, picture it in the mind as a design. The picture can be redesigned by reshaping components, or making fresh arrangements of them. Gaps can be noticed, interrelationships perceived, functions of components contemplated, and limitations questioned. Rough diagrams may help, perhaps using symbols for the various factors.

The fifth precept is to break down the problem into separate parts. This is different from conventional analysis which is a systematic, complete fractionation aimed at explanation. Instead, the purpose here is to identify parts in order to rearrange them, to restructure the problem. The reassembling should avoid putting the parts back into the same positions, which would only lead back to the original impasse. An attempt should be made to reverse the parts and to shuffle them around.

The sixth precept is to seek random stimulation from outside the problem. There are several ways of doing this, for example wandering around a large general store like Woolworths or a toy shop just looking about, or selecting a word at random from a dictionary. In wandering around the store one does not look for something directly relevant to the problem, that would only reinforce one's present ideas. One should keep the mind blank and wait for something to catch one's attention. The random object, or the word from the dictionary, starts off a flow of associated ideas and one of these may by a lucky chance throw light on the problem.

The seventh precept is to take part in a brainstorming session. This procedure is described later.

THE MORPHOLOGICAL APPROACH

This is the name given to a method of solving problems and inventing things devised by Dr Fritz Zwicky, professor of astrophysics at the California Institute of Technology and one-time director of research at the Aerojet Engineering Corporation. The method is described at length in Zwicky's book *Discovery, Invention, Research*, and a more succinct description and evaluation of it is given by Delp and co-authors.[25,104]

In brief, the morphological method comprises the following steps:

(a) The problem is defined precisely.

(b) A list is made of the basic components or factors involved in the problem ('elements'); these are material objects and theoretical concepts that are included in the definition or are seen to be closely relevant; for example the elements of an agricultural problem might include land use, climate, soil, population, etc. The list should be as comprehensive as possible and the elements should, where necessary, be defined, or at least be definable.

(c) For each element a subsidiary list is made of every form, character or dimension that it could assume ('attributes'). For example, if an element is energy source, its attributes could be oil, gas, solar, nuclear, fuel cell, wind, water, etc. Again the list should be as exhaustive as possible.

(d) The elements and their attributes are tabulated in what Zwicky calls a morphological box or multidimensional matrix. The elements are listed vertically down the side, and opposite each are written horizontally its attributes.

(e) The elements, being basic to the problem, are fixed; but the attributes, being alternatives, are not. All possible combinations of the attributes are synthesized and then each is thoroughly scrutinized and appraised as a possible solution to the problem. Even illogical combinations are considered, as they may trigger feasible alternatives.

This recipe for problem solving has two main virtues: its comparatively exhaustive nature reduces the risk of novel significant combinations being overlooked, and, since the synthesis of possible solutions is done systematically and objectively, the blocking effect of conventional thinking and prejudice are avoided. According to Zwicky the morphological approach has extraordinary suggestive power and has been used with great success over twenty-five years in a wide variety of technological, scientific, and social spheres.

GROUP THINKING

Group discussion has certain advantages in addition to the

obvious one, that the pool of knowledge available is greater than any one individual's resources. There is a greater variety of information and of intellects; exchanging information and ideas is stimulating and it leads to cross fertilization; there is an enlivening atmosphere that inspires enthusiasm; successes, disappointments, and frustrations are shared. However, group activities should not be thought of as a substitute for individual effort, but rather as supplementing and inciting it. Intellectual intercourse is most productive in small groups of not more than half a dozen or so.

Scientists have long been aware of the value of group discussions. Scientific conferences and 'workshops' are an important part of the scientific life, and it is a common practice in most research laboratories to hold small informal meetings every week or two where the current research is discussed in a relaxed atmosphere. At the Molecular Biology Laboratory in Cambridge Dr Francis Crick and Dr Sidney Brenner used to keep a sort of running discussion going on a blackboard.[94] Recent results from their own and other laboratories were stated briefly at the top. Under this a series of comments, criticisms and implications were noted; these were added to or modified by colleagues from time to time.

In the USA during the 1950s more elaborate group activities were developed for the express purpose of generating new ideas, based on the principles of wild thinking. Two techniques, brainstorming and synectics, have been widely taken up by commercial firms and by the US Armed Forces.

In a brainstorming session a group of from three to fifteen people—ideally six to twelve—spend twenty to forty-five minutes discussing a subject. There are certain rules to be observed, so a chairman is appointed to keep control, and a secretary to keep a record. The objective is to throw up new ideas under the stimulus of the interaction of minds, but without any attempt at appraisal or criticism. The chairman introduces the problem and perhaps indicates in general terms the sort of solution being sought, and he then invites suggestions. Even the wildest ideas are welcomed, and instead of criticizing or rejecting them, participants try to improve on them or develop new lines of thought from them. This provokes people to look at the problem in a new way. A positive, helpful and optimistic attitude is essential, and spontaneity and friendly competitiveness are encouraged. The chairman keeps order, prevents the discussion from wandering too far from the subject, and sees that each suggestion is noted down.

The meeting is closed before the subject is exhausted and the participants fatigued. Members often continue to have ideas after the session and these are sent to the secretary.

A second session is held to evaluate the suggestions that have been produced. This may consist of the same participants or have a new membership. The purpose is to sort out the potentially useful ideas from the obviously wrong or ridiculous, and to try to refine them to the point where they can be tried, or used as a basis for the collection of more information that may throw light on the subject. The evaluation session does more than just select the grain from the chaff, it is constructive. While wild thinking is the medium of the first session, critical thinking prevails in the second. Finally three lists are drawn up: (a) ideas that can be applied straightaway, or at least tried out; (b) aspects of the subject that require further investigation, and (c) possible fresh approaches to the problem, or around the difficulty, for further consideration.

A development from the brainstorming session is a procedure known as '6–3–5' brainstorming. Six people each write three ideas on a card, which they pass to another member of the group, who in turn tries to build on the original idea. The cards are passed five times, so that each of the six members has a chance to add constructive thoughts to everyone else's suggestions.

Synectics is the name given to a system that uses the techniques of brainstorming in a special way. The word synectics, derived from Greek, means joining together different and apparently unrelated elements, in this case bringing together people with diverse backgrounds to form a problem-solving group. Dr William J. J. Gordon was primarily responsible for organizing a group at Cambridge, Massachusetts, linking personnel from academic institutions with those from industry. Its purpose was to investigate the nature of the creative process by studying the way people's minds work while solving problems, and thus identify mental techniques that can be taught and practised. The following are some of the techniques found useful and adopted by Gordon and his associates in group sessions, in which not more than five or six people take part.

In order to escape from accepted ways of looking at familiar things a conscious effort is made to see them in a new light: one of the best ways of doing this is to learn to play with metaphors. Four ways of stimulating the imagination along these lines are to make use of (a) personal analogy, (b) direct analogy, (c) symbolic analogy, and (d) fantasy analogy. By personal analogy is meant imagining oneself as one of the key components of the problem. Direct analogy is relating the problem to a comparable situation in another context. The richest sources of parallel situations productive of ideas are to be found in biology; the infinite variety found in nature can often be useful in indicating possible solutions to mechanical problems. Symbolic analogy uses poetic imagery; the image may be scientifically inaccurate but aesthetically pleasing. In fantasy analogy members of the group let their fantasy run wild and picture in their minds quite fanciful situations, for example having a team of insects working under one's direction, or having magical powers as in fairy tales.

It is not possible to describe here the various psychological tools that the synectics group have found productive. Readers interested in pursuing the subject further are recommened to study Gordon's *Synectics. The Development of Creative Capacity*.[42] Synectics theory is based on the belief, borne out by experience, that creative ability can be cultivated by practising methods that have proved fruitful.

Under the heading of group thinking, mention should be made also of the Delphi technique, although it is not designed to produce new ideas so much as to obtain a consensus of opinions on controversial subjects or on predicting likely future developments. In this method opinions are sought by letter from selected experts on a particular question. The replies are summarized or tabulated and the whole collection sent back to each participant for further comment and perhaps revision of his original opinion. This process may be repeated if necessary until a conclusion is reached by the majority on the main points. The Delphi method has the advantage that during the first round each participant gives his views without being influenced in any way by the others, as would occur if the experts were brought together at a meeting. During subsequent rounds there is an opportunity for interplay of views and possible emergence of new ideas.

★   ★   ★

At the end of this chapter, lest I be charged with encouraging the adoption of wild ideas, I would remind the reader that the discussion has been about ways of producing new ideas irrespective of their validity; once found they must always be examined by disciplined, critical thinking before being promulgated or accepted as a basis for action. Also I should correct any impression I may have given unintentionally that creative thinking in science is mainly concerned with searching for fresh meaningful combinations of *old* pieces of information. In fact the researcher spends most of his time carrying out experiments and observations to obtain *new* information and combining that with the old. But the mental techniques are the same whether the information available is new or old. Creation, making new ideas from available information, should not be confused with discovering new factual information, which is quite another matter. We come to that in the next Chapter.

2

Chance and opportunism

'Adventure on, for from the littlest clue
Has come whatever worth man ever knew'
JOHN MASEFIELD

THE ROLE OF CHANCE

Most discoveries that break new ground are by their very
nature unforeseeable, therefore almost the only way of making
such a discovery is by stumbling across some clue to it
inadvertently. As Arthur Koestler has put it in his picturesque
style, the history of discovery is full of arrivals at unexpected
destinations, and arrivals at the right destination by the wrong
boat.

Philosophers of science have failed to appreciate the cardinal
role that chance and opportunism play in research, and most
have dismissed the subject as hardly worthy of their serious
consideration. They regard fortuitous events and observations
as merely of anecdotal interest and not part of the 'scientific
method'. But experienced, successful scientists take a different
view. Let me call as witnesses three eminent modern scientists,
all Nobel Laureates, one in chemistry, two in medicine. Sir
Cyril Hinshelwood: 'Again and again the key to a great
discovery has been an unexpected observation.'[50] Sir Macfarlane Burnet: 'In all areas of science, chance and a questioning
mind are liable to be more important than logic and
perseverance.... In biology, serendipity has always played a
major role.'[13] Sir John Eccles: 'This is essentially the way in
which I have made discoveries. They arose from the happenings
that I was not expecting, where eventually I was tuned in
enough to listen to what nature was trying to tell me. The good

. . . research workers are those who can recognize and appreciate the significance of the unexpected.'[31]

In my earlier book on scientific investigation I treated chance as a factor of great significance and pointed out ways in which the researcher can profit by realizing the part it plays.[8] These views have been well received in scientific circles, so I am encouraged to develop the subject further here.

In analysing the part that chance plays in science, one can distinguish three different types of discovery in which it is the vital factor: an intuition from random juxtaposition of ideas, a eureka intuition, and serendipity. The origin of the first is entirely mental, the second arises from interaction of mental activity with the external world, the third is found externally without an active mental contribution.

By intuition from *random juxtaposition of ideas*, I mean the sudden linking of apparently unconnected ideas or pieces of information in the mind to form a new, meaningful relationship. Procedures such as brainstorming have been devised for the express purpose of throwing up a multitude of ideas indiscriminately, thus providing opportunities for novel, significant associations to be formed and grasped. This role of chance in purely mental activities has already been discussed in Chapter 1.

In a *eureka intuition* the scientist observes some rather common event and suddenly perceives the analogy between it and some aspect of the problem he has been puzzling over: this triggers off a flash of illumination in a mind already loaded with a mass of relevant information. The casual observation provides the nucleus for crystallization of vague thoughts that have been floating about in the mind, perhaps largely unconsciously. The two classical examples are the Archimedes story already mentioned, and Isaac Newton watching an apple fall from a tree and perceiving the parallel between it and the moon being attracted by the gravity of the earth. De Bono's sixth precept in lateral thinking, seeking random stimulation from outside the problem, is a way of deliberately seeking a eureka intuition. I have followed the same principle myself by just looking around me, wherever I may be—occasionally with success.

In *serendipity* the scientist encounters an unusual event, or a curious coincidence of two not unusual events, or an unexpected experimental result. There is no question here of clinching already half-formed ideas, or seeing suggestive analogies, because the observed event is itself the discovery, or a strong clue to it; it comes as a surprise and it may be met with doubt or even incredulity. Whereas a eureka intuition evokes the exclamation 'I have found it', that is, a solution fervently sought, in serendipity the reaction is quite different— something is found that was *not* being looked for. It is not an intuition. Two classical examples are Columbus finding the New World while seeking the Orient, and von Röntgen's discovery of X-rays, which few believed at first. Serendipity is defined in three dictionaries I consulted as 'the gift of finding valuable things in unexpected places by sheer luck', 'the faculty of making happy and unexpected discoveries by accident', and 'an assumed gift for finding valuable and agreeable things not sought for'. The word serendipity was coined by Horace Walpole in 1754 after reading an ancient oriental fairy tale about three Princes of Serendip. Walpole wrote: 'they were always making discoveries, by accidents and sagacity, of things which they were not in quest of ... you must observe that *no* discovery of a thing you *are* looking for comes under this description.'

In all three of these situations, chance is only one factor, though a vital one. It merely provides the opportunity. The scientist has to notice the clue, realize its possible significance, and follow it up: this requires a special talent.

So much then for the general principles. Let us examine some case histories to see exactly how chance was involved in particular discoveries.

ILLUSTRATIVE ANECDOTES

The discovery of penicillin, the father of all antibiotics, provides a supreme example of the part that chance may play, because it was the outcome of a whole series of unlikely events. Sir Peter Medawar has referred to penicillin as the greatest single advance in medicine in the twentieth century, so it is a good example for us to examine.[70] The story often told by Sir Alexander Fleming himself does not reveal all the circumstances; these only came to light much later when a colleague, Dr Ronald Hare, re-investigated the whole matter. The remarkable combination of circumstances that led to the discovery is told in his fascinating book *The Birth of Penicillin*.[47] It will disillusion anyone who still believes that making discoveries is a purely rational process. The following is a brief outline of the story.

During the First World War Fleming was one of a team of doctors who worked on the bacteriology of war wounds. They found that the antiseptics then available were useless for killing bacteria in deep wounds; in fact they did more harm than good, because they severely damaged the exposed tissues. It was obvious that what was needed was a substance more lethal to bacteria than to tissues. Fleming was one of several who continued for years to look for such an antiseptic. He found an antibacterial substance called lysosyme present in tears, but it proved to be of no use against those bacteria that cause disease. It has been said with justice that Fleming discovered penicillin because he was constantly looking for something to kill bacteria.

In 1927 Fleming was working with disease-producing bacteria called staphylococci, growing them on solid gel in round glass dishes. During August he went for a vacation; before going he piled the culture dishes on his bench and left them there. The normal thing to do would be either to put them in the refrigerator or to discard them, but Fleming was not tidy or systematic. When he returned in September he looked at the cultures again and discarded them in a shallow tray with Lysol in the bottom. Just then his colleague, Dr D. M. Pryce, came into the laboratory and asked how the work was going. To demonstrate a point, Fleming took up some of the cultures already discarded but luckily not submerged in the Lysol. Some were contaminated with moulds, which commonly happens under these conditions. One culture in particular attracted Fleming's attention; after looking at it a while, he said 'That's funny'. Some of the staphylococci colonies near a mould colony had been lysed, that is, they had become

Sir Karl Popper

Jacques Monod

Edward de Bono

Arthur Koestler

transparent because the bacteria had been broken down. Fleming and Pryce discussed the observation and agreed it was very odd, and Fleming made a subculture of the mould. The now famous culture was shown to several colleagues, but most of them were not interested.

Until Hare re-investigated the matter and tried to 'rediscover' penicillin, it had been assumed that what Fleming saw was a not uncommon phenomenon that others must have seen and ignored. The truth is quite different. Fleming himself tried many times to 'rediscover' penicillin, but never succeeded. Ordinarily penicillin does not lyse staphylococcal colonies; it prevents them from developing, but if added after they have developed it has no apparent effect. Hare found that it was very difficult indeed to reproduce lysis of staphylococcal colonies, even when the cultures were deliberately inoculated with a known penicillin-producing mould. Only after a long series of experiments was he able to discover the very special conditions required to produce the phenomenon. He showed that the rare oddity that Fleming observed could only have arisen as a result of a chain of events that produced just the right, unusual conditions. Fleming must have inoculated a culture dish which at the same time became accidentally contaminated with a mould spore, and instead of putting it in the incubator as is normal practice, it seems he must have got it mixed up with old cultures and inadvertently left it on the bench. The dish lay there during Fleming's vacation and it so happened that there was an unseasonably cold snap in the weather that provided the particular temperature required for the mould and the staphylococci to grow slowly and produce lysis of the staphylococci colonies near the mould colony. Hare remarks that the odds against this combination of unlikely events happening just by accident, which of course it did, must be astronomical.

Yet another extraordinary circumstance was that the particular strain of the mould on Fleming's culture was a good penicillin producer although most strains of that mould, Penicillium, produce no penicillin. Some time later American researchers made a world-wide search for strains capable of producing a high yield of penicillin: Fleming's original strain was one of the three best producers. Hare's investigations show that this strain probably came, not 'through the window' as Fleming supposed, but up the stairwell from a laboratory just below Fleming's, where research on moulds happened to be going on at the time.

The story does not end there. Fleming tried to produce penicillin in a form in which it could be used to treat infections, and he did treat a few cases by external application. But there were all sorts of difficulties and obstacles and eventually he gave up. Neither he, nor anyone else at the time, imagined the great potential of penicillin as a therapeutic agent. Everyone concerned was aware that some other antibiotics had been discovered before, but had proved useless for treating disease. For about nine years nothing further was done about it, and then, possibly stimulated by the onset of war and the urgent need to find an effective way of combating infections in wounds, Sir Howard Florey and his team in Oxford University re-investigated the possibility of producing penicillin in a form in which it could be used to treat infections. They managed to overcome the chemical problems and in 1940 succeeded in producing penicillin that could be used not only as a local application to wounds but which could be administered systemically and gave remarkable cures in many types of infection. Another extraordinary feature of this discovery is that penicillin is still one of the best and most widely used antibiotics, despite the fact that many, many millions of dollars have been spent deliberately searching for antibiotics since the principle was established by Fleming and Florey and colleagues some forty years ago.

I think we can include under the heading of serendipity those discoveries that start from an observation of a lay person that the scientist takes notice of and follows up. Jenner's epoch-making work on vaccination is said to have been initiated by a remark of one of his patients, Sarah Nelmes, whom he thought might be sickening from smallpox. She said 'No, I cannot take smallpox because I have had cowpox'. A more recent example is the discovery that rubella in pregnant women can cause congenital defects in babies. This discovery is attributed to Sir Norman Gregg, an Australian ophthalmologist. It happened that two clients in his waiting room both had babies with congenital cataracts; when one came into his office she asked what was the cause, could it perhaps be rubella, which she had had in early pregnancy? Gregg said he did not think so. But the mother told him that there was another woman in the waiting room whose baby was similarly affected and she also had had rubella. Gregg was astute enough to take the suggestion seriously and on searching his records he found other instances of the coincidence of rubella and congenital cataracts.[45] His report in the medical literature met with much scepticism and only after several years of extensive investigation was it possible to convince the medical profession that this disease, hitherto regarded as trivial, caused congenital defects. Infection in early pregnancy causes not only cataracts, but also cardiac abnormalities, deafness and mental retardation. These tragedies can now be prevented by vaccinating girls before pregnancy.

Congenital defects in babies are much more common than is generally realized, and in most cases the cause is unknown. One of the saddest tragedies that can befall a mother and father is to produce a baby that is severely handicapped for life, physically or mentally. Gregg's research led to the prevention of some such cases, but unfortunately there are still enormous numbers due to unknown causes and therefore not preventable. Another discovery that may help in this field was made a few years ago by Dr Marshall Edwards of Sydney. He was in charge of the colony of guinea-pigs at the Veterinary School. The animal house was being rebuilt and the guinea-pigs were housed temporarily in a galvanized iron building during the summer. Edwards noticed that some baby guinea-pigs were born with deformities of various sorts. Instead of dismissing the incident as of little importance, he tried to find out what had caused the abnormalities. Eventually he tracked it down to the high temperature the pregnant females had been exposed to in the temporary building. He followed up this discovery with a long series of experiments investigating the mechanisms involved. One especially interesting finding was that baby guinea-pigs that had been exposed to only moderately high temperatures while in their mother's womb and showed no very obvious deformity, in fact had brains that were somewhat smaller than normal. Moreover, when these animals became adults, they were found to perform subnormally in psychological tests. Edwards's research has led to experimental studies in other animals, including monkeys, where essentially similar results are being obtained. Epidemiological studies in human beings are now under way and already some cases of congenital defects in babies have been found that can be attributed to the mother having been exposed to high temperature or having had a fever during early pregnancy.[33,34,73]

One of the most important advances in immunology of recent years has been the recognition that there are two different lymphocyte systems, one of which produces antibody and the other cellular immunity. Serendipity played a key role in the discovery of each of the two systems. The antibody-producing system was the first recognized. Some twenty-five years ago Dr B. Glick and colleagues in the USA were studying the effect of hormones on the growth rate of chickens. In the course of this investigation they surgically removed various organs, including the bursa of Fabricius, from newly hatched chicks. These bursectomized chicks appeared to develop normally and were set aside as of no interest. Some months later they were used for another purpose; they were inoculated with a bacterial culture as a class demonstration, but surprisingly they were found to produce practically no antibody. Glick looked into the reasons for this unexpected result and eventually found that removal of the bursa soon after hatching deprived chickens of the ability to produce antibody. Lymphocytes can produce antibody only after they have been prepared by the bursa, which was thus recognized as a key organ in the immune system.[13, 41] A few years later it was found that there exists a separate lymphocyte system not concerned with the bursa or antibody production, but with cellular immunity. This discovery was made by an Australian, Dr J. F. A. P. Miller, while doing research on leukaemia in mice. It was known that surgical removal of the thymus gland in young adult mice prevented them from developing leukaemia, and that they suffered no ill effects from having no thymus. Miller wondered what the effect would be if the thymus was removed soon after birth and he developed a clever technique for doing this. These mice did not develop leukaemia, but soon after weaning they developed various infections and died. 'Analysing the situation, Miller soon realized that he had come, by serendipity, on to the real function of the thymus. Far from being an organ of antibody production, the thymus is a school where young lymphocytes are trained in their task of becoming immune defenders (killer cells) ... Thus Miller, a cancer research worker, revolutionized immunology overnight in 1961'.[77]

The following story concerns the ecology of influenza virus. During the 1960s in a number of places strains of influenza virus were isolated from sick domestic poultry and some wild birds. In most instances these strains caused disease of the respiratory tract in the birds as other strains of influenza virus do in man, and in all animals known to be susceptible (horses, pigs, and ferrets). The bird strains did not seem to be virulent for man, nevertheless it was thought they may play a significant part in the epidemiology of human influenza. Therefore extensive investigations were undertaken, especially in the USSR and in the USA, in order to study the ecology of the virus in wild birds, as these were apparently the source of the infection of domestic poultry. Thousands of wild birds were captured or shot and swabs taken from the respiratory tract and examined for virus, and a number of isolations were made. But this was only the tip of the iceberg, as was later shown by quite a different investigation. In 1971 there were outbreaks of severe Newcastle disease of chickens in California. It was suspected that the Newcastle virus may have been introduced in cage-birds imported from the Orient where that disease was known to occur. Therefore Dr Richard Slemons and colleagues examined imported birds for the virus. Now, in testing birds for Newcastle virus the normal procedure is to examine their faeces by taking swabs from their cloaca. Some isolations of Newcastle virus were in fact made as expected, but, more important, Slemons also found quite a number of influenza viruses in the faeces from birds that appeared normal. Until then, influenza virus had always been looked for in the respiratory tract because that is the only part of the body where it can be found in man, horses, and pigs. Following

Slemons's findings, the influenza hunters turned their attention to bird faeces. The result has been the isolation of hundreds of strains from many species of wild and domestic birds showing no illness. It now seems that the natural home of the influenza virus is the gut of birds, a situation undreamt of just a few years ago.[10]

The story of Dr Charles Nicolle's discovery that typhus is transmitted by lice is an example of a eureka intuition. He was working in Tunis during an outbreak of typhus. He had been puzzled by the fact that, although the disease spread readily from person to person in the town, for some unknown reason there was no risk of contagion from cases in the hospital. One day as Nicolle entered the hospital he saw a native who had collapsed with typhus near the doorway—a not uncommon sight at the time. As he stepped over the prostrate form, it came to him in a flash that the reason why hospital patients did not pass on the infection was that they were first shaved and bathed; their capacity to transmit typhus was thereby removed. He realized this could only be because they had been rid of lice. Nicolle relates that he felt absolutely convinced this was the answer, and he went on to prove it by experiments in monkeys.[76]

The 1978 Nobel Prize for Physiology and Medicine was awarded for a discovery that owed much to serendipity. Dr Werner Arber of Basel University, Switzerland and Drs Daniel Nathans and Hamilton Smith of Johns Hopkins University, Baltimore, USA, shared the prize for their discovery of restriction endonucleases, which have proved an invaluable tool in research in molecular biology. These bacterial enzymes have made it possible to dissect and analyse the genetic material (genomes) of microbes and thereby have opened up new avenues in recombinant DNA research (a form of genetic engineering). During the 1960s the first restriction enzymes were recognized; they cleaved viral genomes at random positions and so were of little use for research on the structure of genes. Then in 1970 a second type of restriction enzyme was discovered that cleaved genes at highly specific points; these proved to be the keys to the secrets of the structure of the DNA genome; they have revolutionized research in molecular biology and led to an explosive burst of knowledge. At the practical level these enzymes enable diagnostic virologists to 'fingerprint' particular strains of many viruses, and this provides an invaluable tool for epidemiologists in tracing the source of infections. Initial detection of the so-called Type II restriction enzymes was described by the authors as a chance discovery.[84]

These eight examples are all drawn from the field of medical science, since that is the field with which I am most familiar, but serendipity is no less important in other branches of science. Here is an example from astrophysics. Two radioastronomers, Dr A. A. Penzias and Dr R. W. Wilson, working in 1965 in New Jersey, developed a new apparatus to detect weak radiowaves from extra-terrestrial sources. Their aim was to measure the intensity of microwaves emitted from certain parts of our galaxy. To their surprise, they detected an appreciable amount of microwave activity that was not related to any particular part of the sky, time of the day, or season of the year. They looked for possible sources of error in their equipment, but were quite unable to explain the mysterious microwaves that they continued to receive. After discussion with other astronomers they were led to conclude that what they had discovered was no less than the background of radio 'noise' left over from the beginning of the universe some fifteen billion years ago—the 'big bang'—a sort of fossil microwave.

Astrophysicist Dr Steven Weinberg, writing of this discovery in 1977, remarked: 'The detection of the cosmic microwave radiation background in 1965 was one of the most important scientific discoveries of the twentieth century. Why did it have to be made by accident?' The technology for detecting it was available at least ten years earlier and in fact some theorists had predicted it in 1948. However, the theory predicting it was controversial and there was poor communication between the theorists and the experimentalists. Also the 'big bang' theory itself contained many uncertainties. But Weinberg thinks the main obstacle was that it was extraordinarily difficult to take seriously *any* theory of the origin of the universe; it was hard to believe that the abstruse mathematics referred to real events. He concluded: 'I do not think it is possible really to understand the successes of science without understanding how *hard* it [science] is—how easy it is to be led astray, how difficult it is to know at any time what is the next thing to be done.'[97] Weinberg looks on the story as an illustration of a failure, a missed opportunity on the part of the theorists, who did not have enough confidence in their work to ask the experimentalists to look for the microwaves whose existence they predicted. But I suggest that another way of looking at it is as showing the shortcomings of theory and logic as a means of making breakthroughs, and the rewards of serendipity.

CULTIVATING AN APTITUDE FOR SERENDIPITY

These stories are recounted here not just for their intrinsic interest, but to show the way in which some discoveries involving chance have been made. I am well aware that anecdotal evidence is generally regarded with scorn; it has been brought into disrepute by advertisements that make claims for remedies based on the *post hoc, ergo propter hoc* fallacy. But historically true anecdotes describing circumstances in which new knowledge has been won are instructive and worthy of serious examination.

Researchers should try to cultivate an aptitude for serendi-pity, because discoveries in which chance plays a significant part are not rare oddities, but comparatively common. There are no doubt many unrecognized truths of nature constantly around us awaiting the informed, aware and imaginative person to discover them.

Dr Robert Good, famous American immunologist and director of the Sloan-Kettering Cancer Institute in New York, said: 'For years I have been trying to teach my students that opportunism is a real way of science. If you pay attention to things that don't fit, you are much more likely to make dis-coveries than if you try to find out things that do fit.'[85] In a recent book, Dr James Austin discusses at length the important role of serendipity in research.[2]

In this series of nine cases, Nicolle's discovery was the only example of a eureka intuition. The event he observed was not uncommon, but it supplied the spark for an intuition in his prepared mind. The other cases are examples of serendipity, surprising discoveries. There are several points to note. The scientists were all themselves personally in close contact with the subject concerned; they were not the sort of scientists who sit behind a desk and supervise technicians. Most of the starting points were events seen by visual observation— Fleming's culture, Edwards's deformed guinea-pigs. However, in the case of rubella it was not a visual observation but a mental one: what was noticed was the coincidence between rubella and cataract, neither of which alone supplied the clue. All the scientists were knowledgeable about the subject and so were able to recognize that what they saw was unusual, inexplicable by current knowledge and therefore probably of significance. Moreover, they possessed both the curiosity and the ability to investigate the phenomenon.

'That's Dr Arnold Moore. He's conducting an experiment to test the theory that most great scientific discoveries were hit on by accident.'
Drawing by Hoff; © *1957*
The New Yorker Magazine, Inc.

In addition to the nine examples given here, there are twenty-nine in my earlier work on the subject. These are by no means the only ones that have come to my attention, but they provide enough material from which to draw lessons. Remember Walpole said serendipitous discoveries were made 'by accidents and sagacity'; to attribute them *purely* to chance, that is to say luck, is to miss the point.

Opportunities occur most often with scientists who devote much time to bench or field work, thereby exposing themselves to the likelihood of 'a happy accident' happening to them, for this is where they occur. People who are not explorers and venturesome do not inadvertently happen across new worlds.

As Professor Nikolaas Tinbergen remarked at the Kronberg symposium, the successful observer is he who not only watches closely, but wonders while he watches.[63] This early stage of the investigation requires quite a different attitude of mind from that used later when testing hypotheses.

Many researchers have remarked that prolonged close contact with the phenomenon under investigation has provided an opportunity to observe small but significant details, and also it has given a deeper insight into the nature of the problem.

Only those with a good knowledge of the subject they are working on are likely to recognize something as odd and possibly of interest. And even after the clue has been noticed and the researcher's curiosity aroused, the interpretation of it, finding out what lies behind it, often requires a long and diligent investigation. We have seen the difficulties that Fleming ran into and which he was not able to overcome.

Introspective people who take little notice of their surroundings and are insensitive to them usually miss things of interest. Similarly, researchers who are deeply engrossed in following their programme of work toward a set goal, or concentrating on trying to establish the correctness of their hypothesis, are not likely to notice, or to bother about, small clues that may be exposed in the course of their work. They are not 'accident prone', and in any case they have no time to deviate from the programme they are following. Serendipity is not for them. Fleming told me that he was just 'playing about' when he discovered penicillin, by which he meant that he was not working on a planned research programme. Nowadays grant-giving bodies usually require a fairly detailed plan of work before they will fund a project; this is a strong disincentive to 'playing about'. One must try to strike a balance. While climbing a mountain, one can pause occasionally to examine interesting wild flowers noticed on the way.

However, by no means all clues are worth following; many lead nowhere or only in a direction where one cannot follow owing to the limits of present knowledge. Experience, a good knowledge of the subject, and scientific taste are the only guiding factors for deciding which clues are probably significant.

3

The test of time

'Time reveals the truth'
SENECA, AD 43

THE EMERGENCE OF DISCOVERIES

It is commonly believed that the act of discovery is a sudden event, arising either from a flash of intuition, or a serendipitous observation, or the outcome of one experiment. But in fact it is only the *conception* of new knowledge that occurs suddenly; usually this is followed by a long and often difficult gestation of confirmation and development, so that only gradually does the discovery come to maturity.

After the conception the researcher usually has to perform a number of experiments or systematic observations to establish its truth to his own satisfaction, often after modification of the original idea. Commonly this stage of the work takes months or even years. If the discovery involves some really novel idea, it is generally greeted with indifference, scepticism or perhaps active opposition, even after the researcher has convinced himself of its validity. The discovery is widely accepted only after the work has been repeated successfully by others.

Advances, especially new theories, are seldom so straightforward that they can be verified by a few experiments. A normal course of events is for a new hypothesis to be put forward on incomplete evidence. It is important to remember this, and not rule out the notion just because the evidence so far available is not convincing. Scepticism is healthy only up to a point. Judgement should be suspended till more investigations have been carried out. Sir Gustav Nossal made a forceful comment on this point. 'In most ... discoveries as they first emerge, there is a sufficient element of doubt and tentativeness to give scope to a stern critic; it is relatively easy for an intelligent man to pick holes in the incomplete but truly new discovery.... The overly critical, highly intelligent but unoriginal scientist can become a negative force in research.'[77] Another writer, Harvey, said 'Every new theory is born surrounded by counter instances and to be successful it has to be protected and nurtured until it gains strength.'[48] Speaking at the Kronberg symposium, Dr Desmond Morris pointed out that the creative act is often full of errors because it is sudden and involves a dramatic shift in thinking. 'We must not expect the innovator to produce something of supreme excellence, but we must be thankful to him for showing us a new direction.'[63] Dr T. S. Kuhn, in his *The Structure of Scientific Revolutions* wrote 'To be accepted as a paradigm, a theory must seem better than its competitors, but need not, and in fact never does, explain all the facts with which it can be confronted.'[64] This is perhaps overstating the case. The philosopher A. N. Whitehead said 'all truly great ideas seem somewhat absurd when first proposed.'

Interpretation of reported new findings depends on one's particular background of knowledge and on one's scientific taste (see Chapter 6). It is a very individual thing. Even the philosopher Sir Karl Popper admits to subjective judgement: 'I freely admit that in arriving at my proposals I have been guided in the last analysis, by value judgements and predilections.'[82] One of the common fallacies that should be avoided is what might be called the fallacy of the only conclusion, that is, to conclude that something must be so because there seems to be no alternative. There may be an alternative no one has yet thought of.

Modest advances made in the mainstream of a rapidly developing field are usually accepted fairly readily, provided they do not conflict with current beliefs. And of course the reputation of the researcher is also a factor—respect for authority is not quite dead! But more important advances involving novel ideas go through a probationary period when evidence is accumulated step by step and gradually more and more scientists become convinced, until eventually the new theory or information is built into the currently accepted body of knowledge and incorporated in text-books. What is not sufficiently realized by the non-scientist is that this process is largely a matter of subjective judgement of the evidence by the scientific community, and it takes time, often several years, for a consensus to be reached.

The explanation behind this long drawn out course of events is that discoveries of consequence are generalizations, i.e. theories arrived at by induction. Experiments and observations, however well conducted, can only establish the truth of past events. On the basis of those data one can say with confidence that in the particular circumstances of the experiment a certain procedure *caused* a certain effect. But, for the theory to be of value, it must be stated as a generalization in the present tense (implying the future), namely, the procedure *causes* the effect in appropriate circumstances, irrespective of time. In order to make the inductive jump from the past to present tense, one needs as a premise a body of evidence collected under a variety of circumstances, and even then there is no certainty. This is a logical problem which will be discussed in the next chapter. However, it is a very real problem in practical science, for example in establishing the efficacy and safety of new products, such as vaccines, drugs, foods, agricultural chemicals, which are in essence the materializations of theories. Many scientists do not give sufficient attention to this problem, but there is one discipline in which it is all too obvious, namely meteorology. Here we see how unreliable are forecasts of future events extrapolated from past evidence. Data collected only an hour or so previously do not enable scientists to foresee what the weather will be even for the next few days with any accuracy.

In most cases there are two types of evidence used in judging a new hypothesis or claim to a factual discovery: the direct evidence of the reported observational data or experimental results that led to the assertion, and the indirect or circumstantial evidence relating it to the general body of knowledge—'explaining' it. Take a very simple assertion as an illustration: if a person's skull is crushed, he will die. The direct evidence is that there are many instances of people dying when their skulls were crushed in accidents. The indirect evidence is the knowledge that the body cannot function when the brain is destroyed. When Uri Geller performed remarkable feats on the television, bending metal objects apparently by sheer will-power, many people believed what they saw—the direct evidence—but they were in a dilemma because they could not reconcile the phenomenon with their general experience and knowledge. New scientific claims are sometimes in much the same sort of situation if they are not consistent with currently held views. Direct evidence may be subject to error or even occasionally to fraud, so it is necessary that one also takes into account indirect evidence; subjective opinion should not be ruled out, except when it is based on prejudice due to irrelevant factors such as personal antipathy to people involved. Obviously the more knowledge one has relevant to the particular subject, the better position one is in to make a correct judgement. Scientific knowledge is not piecemeal, it comprises one integrated whole. When presented with an isolated finding a scientist instinctively tries to integrate it—to 'explain' it, to 'understand' it.

Scientists do not work in isolation. All are members of the world-wide scientific community. It is joined together by communication through scientific journals and meetings, which are an essential part of science. Formal and informal discussions at scientific meetings, sometimes involving conflict of views and arguments, are a feature of the scientific life. These are normally conducted with complete freedom from authoritarianism: the most junior scientist can with impunity voice his criticism of the views of the most senior. This healthy atmosphere does not always prevail in totalitarian countries, to the detriment of science in those countries. The Lysenko affair in the USSR was an extreme case but it shows what can happen under a totalitarian regime when all criticism is stifled. A Russian agronomist, T. D. Lysenko, during the 1930s won the complete support of the authorities—Stalin in particular. He claimed to be able to increase crop yields rapidly by methods which rejected the orthodox principles of genetics and denied the role of the chromosomes. Lysenko was appointed to an influential position and became an autocrat; those who criticized his theories and experiments were secretly arrested. His teachings and unscientific attitudes had a crippling effect on biology in the USSR for thirty years and held back crop development. It was not until the 1960s that he was overthrown and Soviet biology became re-established on a proper scientific basis.[5] Tolerance of adverse criticism is an indispensable part of the scientific process, and science does not flourish when criticism has been suppressed. Today science is handicapped in authoritarian societies except in a few subjects that are richly supported for political reasons.

The practical application of new knowledge also often has to go through a long developmental process, and its successful fulfilment may depend on other advances. Drs Comroe and Dripps have protested against the current teaching of science in schools which perpetuates the oversimplified and misleading concept of one-man discoveries.[16] Not only are discoveries based on past advances, but their fruition often requires contributions from several others besides the originator. Moreover, many discoveries are made independently by two or more scientists because the advance of knowledge had reached the point where the discovery was due to occur. There are also many instances of discoveries that are made and published but not taken up and fully developed till years later. A classical example is Gregor Mendel's work on genetics which was ignored for thirty-five years.

LONG GESTATIONS

As everyone knows, it took a long time to produce enough evidence to convince scientists that there is a causal link between cigarette smoking and lung cancer. Since about 1920 lung cancer has been increasing dramatically, and during the early 1950s data were collected and published in Britain and the USA, showing that cigarette smokers were more commonly affected than non-smokers. These large-scale surveys provided figures which many people accepted as demonstrating that cigarettes cause lung cancer, but there were many sceptics, including one eminent biostatistician. Even later, after masses of data were meticulously collected in prospective studies in several countries, and the statistical association of smoking and cancer was irrefutable, there were still some who said the association was probably incidental and that smokers differed from non-smokers in other respects, such as consumption of alcohol and coffee, and perhaps these other factors were the real cause. There was even a hypothesis advanced, in all seriousness, that the cause was an underlying psychological characteristic which predisposed to both lung cancer and smoking. It took ten years or more before the causal link between smoking and cancer was accepted by all except a few inveterate sceptics.

In 1948 Dr John Cade, a psychiatrist in Melbourne, Australia, discovered that lithium carbonate had a remarkable therapeutic effect on patients with psychotic mania, but nearly twenty years passed before it became widely used. The discovery was a serendipitous one.[14] Cade believed that manic psychosis was due to malfunctioning of the body's biochemistry, and he tested the effect of uric acid from patients on guinea-pigs. The most soluble salt of uric acid is lithium urate, so he used that to make his dilutions. He was surprised to find that the injections had a marked sedative effect on the guinea-pigs. He wondered whether this effect was due to the lithium, so he tried lithium carbonate and found it had a similar action. He then took a bold step; after taking it himself without any ill effects, he administered it to nine patients with manic depression. The effect was quite unprecedented: all the patients were virtually cured and could return to work. But when this important discovery was published in 1949 it aroused little interest. Cade was a little-known government medical officer; manic depression was often intermittent; lithium carbonate was a rather common, very cheap salt and was not promoted by a commercial firm as new drugs normally are. In 1952 chlorpromazine was introduced by a drug firm and soon became widely used in certain psychotic conditions. From then on the great potential of psychotropic drugs in the treatment of mental illness was generally appreciated. In 1953 Danish psychiatrists tried lithium and fully confirmed Cade's results.

In the late 1950s others took it up, but it was not till well into the 1960s that this cheap, highly effective remedy became generally used in the treatment of manic-depressive psychosis.[85] (It has been said that, at one time, if you invented a better mouse trap, the world would beat a path to your door, but this is no longer so; now you have to go out and sell it.)

Lithium not only cures mania and depression, but also prevents attacks in people liable to them. Also it has been found to have a beneficial effect in a number of other types of mental illness and emotional disturbances, especially depression. It is said to be effective in controlling episodic rage in violent criminals in prison. A fascinating finding has been that the waters in certain spas in Europe that have long been used for treating mental illness, some since Roman times, have a high lithium content. But the whole story has not yet been unfolded: research on lithium may well have even more far-reaching consequences. In 1970 Dr E. B. Dawson and colleagues reported the results of an investigation into the lithium content of the municipal drinking water in different towns in Texas. They found that in some parts of the State it is relatively high (100 micrograms per litre), whereas in other parts it is extremely low (2 micrograms); in the towns with very little lithium in the water there is a higher rate of admissions to mental hospitals and a higher frequency of violent behaviour (homicides, suicides) than in the towns where the water is rich in lithium. For example, El Paso has a high level of lithium in the water and has only one-seventh the number of psychiatric admissions that Dallas has, where the lithium content of the water is extremely low.[22] Perhaps lithium is a trace element essential for our mental health, in the same sort of way that iodine is necessary for a healthy thyroid gland and fluorine for healthy teeth. This possibility was in fact suggested by John Cade no less than thirty years ago, but the question has not yet been settled. Dawson raised the question whether lithium should be added to the drinking water in areas where it is deficient.[21] (This brings to mind Arthur Koestler's suggestion that the only way to save mankind from the catastrophic effects of mass emotional aggressiveness and nuclear war is to dose the population with a universal tranquillizer.)[60] However, the idea of influencing people's behaviour by adding substances to the water supply opens up alarming possibilities for dictatorships. Probably this is why the suggestion of putting lithium in the water has not been taken up.

In case it should be thought that science moves faster in the industrial world, here is a story concerning a new method of manufacturing sheet glass. The idea that a flat, polished surface could be produced by floating molten glass on a liquid surface came to Sir Alastair Pilkington when he saw grease solidify on the surface of washing-up water in the kitchen—an instance of a eureka intuition. It took seven years' research and the expenditure of £7 million to find a suitable float bed and to perfect the commercial process using molten tin. It transpired that more than fifty years previously a patent had been taken out for producing sheet glass on the same principle, but it had not been developed into a practical method.[53]

Another technical method that took many years to mature is chromatography. The Nobel Prize was awarded to two English chemists, Dr A. J. P. Martin and Dr R. L. Synge, in 1952 for perfecting this method, which is considered one of the most decisive discoveries of the twentieth century in the field of chemical analysis. Yet the principle involved had been known for more than a century. In 1850 the chemist F. F. Runge analysed mixtures of dyes by dipping the ends of strips of blotting paper into the dye mixture, and he devised several modifications of the technique. In 1861 Schoenbein used paper chromatography for separating metallic salts. In 1901 the Russian, Michael Tswett, used a column of finely ground calcium carbonate to separate the principal constituents of chlorophyll. But Tswett's report was buried in an obscure Russian botanical journal, and in 1931 column chromatography was rediscovered by Kuhn, Winterstein and Lederer. From then on many adaptations of the principle were made, including partition chromatography for which Martin and Synge received the Nobel Prize.[92]

The story of penicillin outlined in the previous chapter provides another good illustration of a slowly maturing discovery. It is the rule rather than the exception for important innovations to take some years to win general acceptance, and for their applications to be developed.

SOME NEGATIVE FACTORS

It is as well to identify some negative forces in science and expose them for what they are. Only the first of those considered here, namely resistance to innovation, is an impediment to discovery and directly relevant to the first part of this chapter. The other two, antiscience cult and pseudoscience, have an adverse effect on science in a more general way. Another negative aspect of science, fraudulent claims, is discussed in the next section.

Resistance to innovation

Indifference to new ideas or active opposition to innovation is a well-known phenomenon which I have already dealt with at some length in my earlier work,[8] so here I shall only mention four examples that occurred this century.

During the first quarter of this century Major Edwin Howard Armstrong made three fundamental inventions to do with radio: regenerative feedback for amplification, super-heterodyne tuning, and frequency modulation for static-free reception. But his methods were contrary to prevailing mathematical theory and he had great difficulty convincing people they worked. 'It is not possible to use the English language to convert people', he said, 'the only way . . . was to build a station, set it up and wipe out by demonstration the things that people knew were not so.' He undertook endless lawsuits to defend his patents; in 1954 he was involved in no less than twenty-one legal disputes and he committed suicide believing he had failed. Thirteen years after his death his legal claims were fully vindicated. The circuits he devised are incorporated in practically all radios today.[54]

When Ludwig von Bertalanffy expounded the general system theory during the 1930s and 1940s, it was received as fantastic and presumptuous. It was described as 'trivial, false, misleading and unsound' and was said to impede analytical research, which was 'obviously' the way in which science has advanced. Then during the next two decades the great significance of the theory became so widely recognized and appreciated that it caused a revolution in some aspects of science (see Chapter 4).[6]

Sir Ronald Fisher was one of the pioneers of modern statistics and designing of experiments. He is now regarded as one of the great scientists of this century, but his early classical paper that laid the foundations of the study of quantitative inheritance was rejected when he submitted it for publication to the Royal Society. Eventually it was published elsewhere, but only thanks to the intervention of a sponsor who met the costs.[11]

Innovators in the scientific world are less likely to be persecuted today than they were in past centuries, but opposition can still be fierce against pioneers of new fields. For example, Dr A. C. Kinsey and Dr W. M. Masters were targets for much abuse when their studies on human sexuality were published. These researchers and their colleagues needed great courage to defy the current taboos. Their work has led to a revolution in attitudes to sexual behaviour and has added greatly to human happiness—or at least reduced unhappiness. Their studies freed people's minds from needless and mentally unhealthy feelings of anxiety, guilt and furtiveness that were associated with some common aspects of sexual behaviour in Western society and caused much unhappiness and sometimes neurosis.

There is also quite another form that an ultra-conservative attitude to the advances of science may take, namely negative predictions, i.e. 'proving' that something not yet achieved is impossible. This can be a check on progress by discouraging scientists from attempting the 'impossible', also by inhibiting financial support. A fascinating account of negative predictions about aeroplanes was published by Dr Eugene Garfield.[40] In 1903 Professor Simon Newcomb published an article that 'proved' that heavier-than-air machines could never fly. Newcomb was professor of mathematics and astronomy at Johns Hopkins University, vice-president of the National Academy of Sciences and held other influential offices. He was a pillar of the Establishment and his authoritative article against attempting to build a flying machine convinced most of his contemporaries of the impossibility of such a project. Newcomb's article was prompted by criticism of attempts by Professor S. P. Langley of the Smithsonian Institute to build a flying machine using government money. Langley's machine was a total failure and the funds were cut off. An editorial in the New York Times said 'For students and investigators of the Langley type there are more useful employments'. However, that very same year, on 17 December 1903, Orville Wright flew for twelve seconds in 'Flyer 1' and landed safely—the first man-carrying, powered flight in history. But, owing to Newcomb's article, several years passed before it was generally believed that the Wright brothers had really flown. In 1906 Newcomb was still convinced mechanical flight was impossible. He wrote: 'The demonstration that no possible combination of known substances, known forms of machinery, and known forms of force can be united in a practicable machine by which men shall fly long distances through the air, seems to the writer as complete as it is possible for the demonstration of any physical fact to be.'

Newcomb was by no means alone in his negative predictions. Lord Kelvin, British physicist and engineer, was equally definite: 'I have not the smallest molecule of faith in aerial navigation other than ballooning.'

After the Wrights had indisputably proved the prophets wrong, they retreated to a new stand. 'The useful loads will be very small. The machines ... are not to be thought of as commercial carriers', one prominent engineer stated. Only eleven years later the first air passenger service began.

Not long ago most scientists and others believed it was not possible for man to travel to the moon, and in 1935 an astronomer, F. R. Moulton, said categorically: 'it must be stated that there is not the slightest possibility of such journeys'. Many astronomers were similarly convinced even much later.

During the great influenza pandemic of 1918–19 and the years that followed, many attempts were made to discover a causal virus, but no-one succeeded. In 1928 Dr W. M. Scott, of the British Ministry of Health, wrote in one of the leading text-books of the time that 'there is little hope that they [the technical difficulties of demonstrating a viral cause] will ever be overcome with influenza'. However, unknown to Scott, about the same time in America Dr Richard Shope was meeting success with his experiments to demonstrate a virus of influenza in swine, and in 1933 Engiish virologists isolated the influenza virus from human cases.[10] I remember reading an article about this time by a leading virologist stating that it would never be possible to produce killed virus vaccines because viruses cannot be cultivated outside the living animal. Only a few years later they were being produced.

When Charles Darwin announced his theory of evolution, it was said to be impossible by one of the leading physicists of the time, Lord Kelvin, on the grounds that the world could not have been in existence for the length of time required by the theory, as the sun would have long since burnt out. This was before the discovery of nuclear fusion which we now know keeps the sun fired.

It may be quite true that a particular goal is impossible today, in light of present knowledge, but unforeseeable break-throughs often occur that make it possible in the future, so negative predictions should always be received with reservations.

It is as well to bear in mind that a pioneer often stands alone. In appraising a report of a revolutionary discovery, or disturbing new idea, the majority is usually wrong. So one should not be influenced too much by the consensus. It is in the nature of things that radical innovation comes from an exceptional individual, who may be on the fringe of the scientific Establishment, independent-minded and perhaps something of a rebel. But of course he too is often wrong!

Another negative attitude that should be mentioned here is pessimism about the future growth of scientific knowledge generally. The belief that all the important discoveries had already been made has cropped up repeatedly throughout history: Aristotle and Descartes in their turn said as much, and the view was widely held towards the end of last century. Now in the last quarter of this century some scientists are again saying the same thing and that science is approaching the completion of its work. To my mind this view is as unjustified now as it was in the past. A vigorous refutation has been given by Dr Nicholas Rescher.[83]

Antiscience
An ideology of antiscience has been developed by some of the New Left movements, who question the validity of scientific thought. This attitude is part of the cult of the rejection of the values of the Establishment by some of the younger generation, but there is more to it than that. Some of the disenchantment with science is the consequence of unfulfilled, excessively optimistic expectations of what science can achieve if only it were given sufficient funds, e.g. a cure for cancer. Some stems from ignorance of the true nature of science, which the disaffected see as entirely rational, objective, technical, and composed of certainties. This is a caricature derived perhaps from elementary teaching in schools and from inept popularization. Science is blamed for all the undesirable aspects of modern technology. More reasonable causes for concern are that our way of life may be changed in undesirable ways, or that, like the sorcerer's apprentice, scientists may create powers that get out of control, for example, in genetic engineering or nuclear physics.

Commenting on these attitudes, Sir Eric Ashby said we should not lightly dismiss this counter culture, especially the pronouncements of the more sophisticated prophets of anti-science such as Ellul and Marcuse, who oppose science on the ground that if its values are adopted mankind will become enslaved by its technology.[1] It would be more correct to say that science itself has no concern with values and is neutral so far as its applications are concerned. It is for society to judge whether or not to accept any particular development as consistent with human aesthetic values, instinctive feelings, and aspirations. Probably most scientists are in sympathy with protests against the false values of a materialistic, consumer society in which advertisers lead the unthinking to believe that happiness lies in acquiring the latest model of automobile or refrigerator. This shallow attitude of mind can only be corrected by more appropriate education and encouragement of the arts and other worthwhile leisure activities. Science and technology, by greatly reducing the need for long hours of laborious work, have freed man for more pleasurable and satisfying activities and at the same time made accessible to the masses cultural activities previously out of their reach. For example, the radio, television, gramophone, and magnetic tape have brought the world's best music within the reach of everyone. Thus technology helps, not hinders, culture.

Reaction to science and technology is discussed in more detail in Chapter 7.

Pseudoscience
By pseudoscience I mean wrongful use of the word science by some cults such as astrology, phrenology, scientology and Christian Science. I shall not comment on these subjects beyond pointing out that, whatever they may be, they are not science in the sense in which that word is generally understood. However, it is not always easy to draw a sharp line between true science and pseudoscience and I venture to suggest that some writings by psychiatrists and psychologists fall in the grey area in-between when they build far-fetched hypotheses that are based on vague concepts and are not testable. Let me give an illustration of what I am referring to. The following quotation is from a paper submitted to the Twenty Third International Congress of Psychiatry, cited by Sir Peter Medawar as a particularly bad example.[70] It is a psychoanalytic interpretation of the role of snakes in the dreams and fantasies of a sufferer from ulcerative colitis. 'The snake represented the powerful and dangerous (strangling), poisonous (impregnating) penis of his father and his own (in its anal-sadistic aspects). At the same time, it represented the destructive, devouring vagina. ... The snake also represented the patient himself in both aspects as the male and female and served as a substitute for people of both sexes. On the oral and anal levels the snake represented the patient as a digesting (pregnant) gut with a devouring mouth and expelling anus.' Elsewhere Medawar sensibly warns against the popular fallacy of accepting writing that is difficult to understand as profound.

DISHONESTY IN SCIENCE

Frauds and cheating occur in science as they do in all human activities, but only very occasionally. There is less scope for fraudulent claims in science than in most walks of life because they are certain to be detected sooner or later.

Probably the most famous scientific fraud was that which later came to be known as the Piltdown hoax. In 1912 Charles Dawson and Arthur Woodward announced that they had discovered a Palaeolithic human skull near Piltdown in Sussex, England. Dawson was a lawyer and amateur archaeologist who lived in Sussex and it was he who produced the first specimens. He took them to Woodward, who worked as a geologist at the British Museum of Natural History. Later they unearthed more bones at or near the same site and on these expeditions Dawson and Woodward were joined by the priest Teilhard de Chardin (who later became famous as the author of *The Phenomenon of Man*). When Woodward and Dawson announced their discovery and displayed their material at a meeting of the Geological Society of London in December 1912, it caused a sensation. The scientific world was excited because the discovery necessitated a revision of the current ideas on the evolution of man; the popular press gave the matter much publicity because the find was made in England where hitherto no remains of early man had come to light, in contrast to France and some other countries which had many finds to their credit.

The remarkable feature of the specimens was that the piece of cranium resembled that of modern man, while the jawbone was like that of an ape. From the start there were a few sceptics who doubted that the two parts had belonged to the same creature, but Woodward and Dawson's reconstruction and interpretation were accepted by most anthropologists, including several eminent ones. Later anthropological discoveries in Africa cast doubt on the authenticity of the 'Piltdown man' and in 1953 the bones were subjected to a sophisticated analysis and shown to be a deliberate fraud. Since then there has been continuous speculation about who was the culprit. All the circumstantial evidence pointed to Dawson and in 1955 a book was written casting strong suspicion on him. However, many of the people concerned did not consider that Dawson had the necessary expertise or access to the materials required, as he was not a professional anthropologist. Woodward was considered an unlikely suspect; he was hated by many people and it was thought more likely that he was the victim against whom the hoax was perpetrated. In 1978 new evidence was revealed by Professor J. A. Douglas, who occupied the chair of geology at Oxford from 1937 to 1950. Shortly before he died at the age of 94, although blind and unable to write, he made a tape recording describing various events and circumstances that led him to believe that his predecessor in the chair at Oxford, Professor Sollas, had been Dawson's accomplice. He said that probably the original intention had been to make a fool of the unpopular Woodward, but the matter got so out of hand that no disclosure was made.[46]

More recently still (April 1979) the whole affair has been reviewed yet again by Stephen Gould.[43] He discounts the evidence implicating Sollas and suggests that Teilhard de Chardin was Dawson's confederate and that they had planned the whole thing as a joke. When it was taken so seriously and caused such a stir, they dared not admit they had faked the specimens. Gould points out that the main interest of the Piltdown hoax is that it shows that even the scientific Establishment can be fooled by evidence that in retrospect is seen to be an obvious fake. He believes that the judgement of English anthropologists was influenced by national prejudice toward accepting an English specimen. Scientists, like other people, are not free from bias due to their culture, hopes and expectations when interpreting evidence.

Another renowned scientific scandal occurred in 1926 and ended with the suicide of the scientist who was accused of fraud. A brilliant but somewhat unorthodox Viennese zoologist, Dr Paul Kammerer, supported Lamarck's theory that some acquired characteristics could be inherited. These views were unfashionable at the time and Kammerer became involved in bitter controversy with the neo-Darwinists, who believed that evolution was due solely to the selection of chance mutations that favour survival. In the early part of this century many biologists became very emotional over these rival theories. Kammerer carried out prolonged breeding experiments with amphibians, but his published results were greeted with scepticism, at least so far as his interpretation was concerned. One particular experiment attracted great publicity, both in scientific circles and in the popular press. This concerned creatures known as midwife toads (Alytes), which normally live on dry land. When Kammerer kept these toads in a watery environment he claimed they developed protuberances on their feet known as nuptual pads and that these were hereditable. Other species of toads that normally live in water do have nuptual pads which enable the male to grasp the wet and slippery female during mating. Kammerer displayed specimens of midwife toads on which he claimed were nuptual pads that had been inherited. It is a tangled and sad story. The English geneticist William Bateson (who coined the term 'genetics') led the attack on Kammerer and hinted that the experiments were faked, although he had no evidence of this. The quarrel rumbled on for several years and finally the storm broke when an American, Dr G. K. Noble, examined a specimen Kammerer had deposited in the Biological Institute in Vienna, and stated in a letter to *Nature* that it was a fake—India ink had been injected where the pads were supposed to be. Having been accused publicly of the worst crime a scientist can commit, Kammerer shot himself. Some forty years later Arthur Koestler carried out a very thorough investigation of the whole story and wrote an interesting book about it called *The Case of the Midwife Toad*.[59] Koestler believes as a result of his extensive enquiries that Kammerer was innocent and that the specimen had been injected by someone else, possibly someone wishing to discredit Kammerer. He depicts him as a tragic figure defeated by the entrenched 'conventional wisdom' of the Establishment.

In 1974 a scientific scandal that received much publicity involved the famous Sloan-Kettering Institute in New York, the largest cancer research institute in the United States.[20] Dr William Summerlin, a dermatologist turned immunologist, claimed to have found a way of transplanting skin from one individual to another, even from one species to another, without it being rejected by immunological processes as normally occurs. This was achieved, he reported, by culturing the piece of skin *in vitro* for some time before grafting it on to the recipient. If true, this was not only of tremendous practical importance, but also of great scientific interest in that it was inconsistent with current immunological theory. Under pressure to produce more experimental evidence in support of his claim, Summerlin produced white mice on which he said he had grafted patches of skin from black mice. But a technician revealed that they were fakes and Summerlin had to admit that he had made the black patches with a felt-tipped pen. Subsequent enquiry revealed that also some of his other reported findings had been fraudulent. The ensuing scandal attracted great attention, especially as the Director of the Institute had sponsored Summerlin and was co-author of some of his publications. There was no suggestion that the Director was involved with the deception, but Summerlin was disgraced and his mental health was in question. The whole incident is described in a book by Joseph Hixson who shows compassion for those involved.[91] He blames mainly the system under which many scientists in the United States work. It imposes tremendous pressure on researchers to produce results, and there is great temptation for them to make exaggerated claims to support applications for grants in a highly competitive atmosphere.

A less blatant way of distorting the truth is to 'improve' the figures obtained in experiments so as to substantiate the expected result. This may vary from frank dishonesty to unconscious bias in subjective interpretation of results. Bias can so easily influence the assessment of results that in medical field trials it is nowadays the practice to conduct them on a 'double-blind' basis, that is neither the patient nor the doctor conducting the clinical trial know which patients receive the drug under trial and which the inactive placebo.

A famous instance of falsification of statistical data occurred in Britain in connection with studies on the hereditability of intelligence. There has been tremendous controversy over the work of the late Sir Cyril Burt, an eminent psychologist, indeed the first ever to receive a knighthood. His findings, published in the 1950s and early 1960s, showed intelligence, as measured by IQ tests, to be highly hereditable and related to social class. His conclusions were accepted by the educational authorities and they formed the basis of certain educational policies. But in 1976 and 1977, after Burt's death, his work was publicly criticized and he was accused of having fabricated his data to support his hypothesis. Most critics agreed that, under scrutiny of modern statistical methods, his data could not be accepted as unbiased and therefore his conclusions were not justified; but whether he was guilty of deliberate deception, unconscious bias, or just carelessness was not clear. Quite recently Dr D. D. Dorfman has re-examined the whole question in detail. He concludes that beyond doubt Burt had fabricated some of the figures that he had presented as observational data, in order to support his beliefs.[27]

Prompted by the Burt affair, the *New Scientist* published a questionnaire on cheating in science, and the replies were analysed by Dr Ian St. James-Roberts.[90] The replies reported over 150 alleged instances of intentional bias. Of these, 74 per cent were said to be due to improper manipulation of data, 17 per cent due to rigging of experiments, 7 per cent to fabrication of experimental data and 2 per cent due to deliberate mis-interpretation. Some of those providing the information admitted that it was not always possible to decide whether bias had been intentional or unintentional.

It is difficult to know how much importance one should attach to the information supplied to the *New Scientist*. There is no way of verifying the allegations, and no indication to what extent the cheating had been carried and how important it was. Even if all allegations were genuine, there is no way of estimating their frequency—do they represent 1 in 100 scientific papers or 1 in 1000?

I cannot agree with St. James-Roberts that the data he analysed provide justification for developing more stringent controls. The present practice is for all research reports submitted for publication to be refereed by one or two experts in the field, and once published they are open to critical examination and the acid test of being repeated in another laboratory. It is a well-established principle in the experimental sciences that no research finding of consequence wins general acceptance until the work has been confirmed by others. The present system provides reasonable safeguards, and to add more checks might lead to suppression of valuable new findings just because they are advanced on evidence judged as unconvincing by referees, or because they are inconsistent with present views.

Finally, it is as well to remember that occasionally genuine errors occur in scientific work. Biological materials do not always behave as expected and instruments can sometimes go wrong. If a scientist finds that he has published a report that contains an error, it is important for him to retract as soon as possible to avoid others being misled—and to save his reputation.

4

Scientific methods

'I believe that there is no philosophical high road in science ... we
are in a jungle and find our way by trial and error, building our
roads behind us as we proceed.'
MAX BORN

THE PHILOSOPHERS' MYTH

In plain English, the phrase 'the scientific method' can only be
taken as meaning the procedures and mental processes used by
scientists in advancing knowledge. Nowadays even some
philosophers admit it is difficult to find a formula that
adequately describes activities characteristic of scientists,
nevertheless the term 'the scientific method' is still widely used.
Many books and innumerable articles have been written about
it, but the strange thing is that the leading authorities on the
subject—Francis Bacon, David Hume, John Stuart Mill, Karl
Popper—have not been scientists. Bacon was a lawyer and the
others professional philosophers. Professor Jacques Monod
said in his *Chance and Necessity* that one must be cautious
about using the word philosophy in the title of a book, or even
in a sub-title, because it will have a distrustful reception from
scientists, and from philosophers a condescending one at best—
so wide is the gap between scientists and philosophers.[74] In
practice scientists hardly ever receive any formal instruction in
the logic of the scientific method during their education, and if
one asks the average scientist what it is, he will probably say
either that he does not know, or that what he has read on the
subject bears little resemblance to research as he knows it.
There are, of course, certain procedures commonly followed
by scientists, as there are in any profession, or indeed any walk
of life, but, as I hope to show in this chapter, it is myth that

scientists follow the set of logical procedures described by philosophers as the scientific method.

Francis Bacon was probably the most influential writer in this field. In his *Novum Organum*, published in 1620, he outlined a doctrine that was accepted for a very long time as a correct account of the procedures to use in advancing scientific knowledge.[3] Stated very briefly in present day language, his method was to collect systematically all relevant information on a subject and arrange it in tables. Often the conclusion then became obvious, but if not, one thought up a number of possible hypotheses and then tested them by experiment to exclude those that were not tenable; the one that survived was affirmed as the truth. He believed this was straightforward and could be used successfully in a routine way by people with no special gifts. At the time this was an extremely important advance, because it put emphasis on acquiring relevant information by observation, looking for new interpretations and testing them by experiment, instead of theorizing from accepted beliefs, mostly from the Classics and Scriptures, as was the custom in those days. Bacon was highly intelligent and made many shrewd comments. But he had no experience as a scientist and did not appreciate the practical difficulties in collecting all relevant information—or even deciding what is relevant—and he failed to understand the inherent uncertainty in interpreting it, that is reaching a correct conclusion by induction. By portraying research as a more or less routine procedure, he neglected the roles of imaginative insight and of serendipity.

The modern view of the scientific method may be summarized as:

(a) recognition and formulation of the problem,
(b) collection of relevant data,
(c) arriving at a hypothesis by induction, indicating causal relations or significant patterns in the data,
(d) making deductions from the hypothesis and testing the correctness of these by experimentation or collection of more data,
(e) reasoning that if the results are consistent with the deduction, the hypothesis is strengthened but not proved.

The above formula is deceptively simple; in fact each stage is fraught with difficulties, both logical and practical, for example:

(a) formulation of the problem may be done incorrectly,
(b) it is difficult to know what data are relevant,
(c) induction is quite unreliable and some modern philosophers deny its existence,
(d) in experimentation there may be practical difficulties and possible sources of error,
(e) usually the results are at best probabilistic, and they may be misleading and open to more than one interpretation.

But the greatest source of misapprehension about the scientific method has been expositions by some writers who distort it by treating just one part of it, e.g. induction, as though it were the whole process: then they show the deficiencies of that part as an account of how science advances. However, this is not the place to attempt a critique of the vast literature on the scientific method, so I shall jump to current views on the subject by the acknowledged authority, Sir Karl Popper.

It is no exaggeration to say that Popper is widely regarded as the greatest living philosopher of science, indeed Nobel Prizewinner Sir Peter Medawar is quoted as saying: 'I think Popper incomparably the greatest philosopher of science that has ever been'.[66] Two other Nobel Prizewinners have also publicly acknowledged his influence on their work: Jacques Monod and Sir John Eccles. In his book *Facing Reality*, Eccles wrote 'my scientific life owes ... much to my conversion in 1945, if I may call it so, to Popper's teaching on the conduct of scientific investigations', and 'I have endeavoured to follow Popper in the formulation and in the investigation of fundamental problems in neurobiology. I think they have enabled me to progress much further and faster in my efforts to understand some operative features of the central nervous system.'[31] He advised scientists 'to read and meditate upon Popper's writings on the philosophy of science and to adopt them as the basis of operation of one's scientific life'. This praise is all the more striking when contrasted with his comments in another context: 'There are lots of books about the methodology of science and also the philosophy of science, but they are mostly wrong and misleading'.

Writing in praise of Popper's philosophy applied to the study of epidemiology, Professor Carol Buck said: 'Had I encountered Popper's writings earlier, I would have done many things differently'.[12] Other eminent scientists and non-scientists have testified to Popper's intellectual influence. His publications have been translated into twenty-one languages and he has received many honorary degrees and other distinguished awards.

After reading these eulogies, one turns to Popper's writings expecting to find a true exposition of the methods of science, a comprehensive strategy that scientists can follow. I regret to say that I have been disappointed.

Popper rejects induction and propounds what is called the hypothetico-deductive system. You start with a hypothesis— either one that is current or one you have thought up—and reason that if it is true then certain consequences (deductions) must follow, and you plan an experiment or series of observations designed to *disprove* them. Thus the hypothesis is tested. If the results are incompatible with the deductions, the hypothesis is modified or rejected; if the results are consistent with them, the hypothesis is corroborated but not proved. Popper's theme is that it is the business of scientists to try to disprove hypotheses, because it is usually possible to disprove them but never to prove them.

In my opinion there are four serious weaknesses in Popper's scheme. My first criticism is that he does not deal with the origin of hypothesis—surely the very heart of scientific discovery. He says there is no such thing as induction and he dismisses creative thinking as outside his field. Popper says:

The work of the scientist consists in putting forward and testing theories. The initial stage, the act of conceiving or inventing a theory, seems to me neither to call for logical analysis nor to be susceptible to it. The question of how it happens that a new idea occurs to a man—whether it is a musical theme, a dramatic conflict, or a scientific theory— may be of great interest to empirical psychology; but it is irrelevant to the logical analysis of scientific knowledge. This latter is concerned not with *questions of fact*, but only with questions of *justification or validity* (his italics).[82]

Nevertheless the title of the book from which this extract is taken is *Logic of Scientific Discovery*, which he describes as the result of an enquiry into the rules of the game of science— that is, scientific discovery. He disowns any obligation to deal with the creative act, with the discovery process itself, yet this is the very thing scientists are striving to do, it is what research is all about! Testing the new idea comes second, and is a function of a lower kind—critical rather than creative. Of course, it is perfectly defensible for a philosopher to confine himself to those aspects of science that are readily dealt with in terms of logic, and to leave the creative aspects to psychologists and others, but the consequence is that the former's writings on discovery appear seriously inadequate to the scientific reader, whose prime interest is in the act of discovery. It is strange that most professional philosophers and psychologists seem to live in separate worlds, despite the fact that it is widely recognized that the union of two disciplines is often very fertile.

A second weakness of Popper's philosophy is that his policy of concentrating on disproving hypotheses, of demolishing theories, is a negative one. No-one would deny that this is one important activity of scientists, but it is not the way most important advances are made. Most of the time a researcher is trying to achieve some objective, or to understand some phenomenon, not to refute some hypothesis. Antibiotics and the helical structure of DNA were not discovered by trying to disprove a theory. As we have already seen in Chapter 3, most new ideas need careful nurturing by seeking supporting evidence; it is only too easy to demolish them at first. And establishing the validity of the idea may be a long and arduous task. Ehrlich battled for years attempting to find substances that would kill disease-producing organisms without damaging the patient. He had faith in his hypothesis that some dyes or drugs could be found that fixed selectively to receptors on microbes. Despite innumerable failures, and the discouraging advice of colleagues, he stubbornly persisted and finally succeeded. He is now revered as the pioneer of chemotherapy. John Snow, now regarded by many as the father of epidemiology, had to struggle in the middle of the last century to get acceptance of his hypothesis that cholera in London was transmitted by swallowing 'the ejections and dejections of cholera patients'. He persisted in the face of contrary evidence, such as that not everyone who drank contaminated water caught the disease. He gathered evidence in favour of his theory that finally led to its acceptance, despite some exceptions that could not be explained in the light of knowledge then available. The history of science abounds with stories of pioneers pursuing a theory, trying to establish it even though much currently available evidence was against it. Indeed any discovery that can be correctly described as revolutionary *must* conflict with current knowledge. Even Popper himself admits 'I am inclined to think that scientific discovery is impossible without faith in ideas which are of purely speculative kind, sometimes quite hazy'.

The central theme of Popperism, as his philosophy has come to be called, is the falsification of hypotheses—or attempts to do so; but this process cannot always be reduced to strict logic, and in my view this is the third weakness in Popper's scheme. It is often difficult to design a really crucial experiment, one that gives a clear-cut yes/no answer. Even a relatively simple proposition, such as the causal connection between smoking and lung cancer, took years to establish. Most experiments in biology and medicine give results in terms of statistical probability of association. Sometimes experimental results are subject to misinterpretation, sometimes they give 'wrong' answers due to the influence of unsuspected or quite unknown factors, or even technical errors. Sir Macfarlane Burnet and other scientists speaking from long experience have warned against too precipitate abandonment of a hypothesis. Theories seldom fit all the facts, there are often awkward exceptions one cannot explain. Sir Peter Medawar said black-and-white distinction between right and wrong belongs more to the schoolroom than the laboratory.[70] Popper is aware of these difficulties and even went so far as to say 'no conclusive disproof of a theory can ever be produced; for it is always possible to say that the experimental results are not reliable', but this weakens the soundness of his emphasis on falsification.

My fourth criticism concerns another of Popper's rules, one that follows from his excessive emphasis on the test of falsification, namely that the only worthwhile hypotheses are those that are susceptible to test and possible refutation. There is of course much to be said for this rule in that scientists should shun hypotheses involving metaphysical or vague, ill-defined concepts that are beyond the reach of experimentation. Nevertheless one must allow exceptions to the rule, because many valuable hypotheses, including some of the most fundamental postulates of science, are untestable. For example, the theory of evolution is not susceptible to disproof although it is one of the basic tenets in biology. New sciences such as sociobiology should not be rejected on the grounds that they contain many flaws; an effort should be made to find grains of truth among the chaff.

Considered purely as philosophy, Popper's writings are impressive and I have no wish to criticize them apart from the point that in my view they do not portray an adequate and realistic description of the way scientists work. I do not think Popper claims they do, but the titles of his books may mislead people into believing so, and a surprising number of scientists have embraced his ideas as guidelines, as we have seen from the statements quoted above. My purpose here is to make this point and to argue that philosophy still has but little to offer in the way of guidance in the practice of research. Of course that is not to say that scientists may not enrich their understanding of the philosophical interpretation of their work by reading Popper, as the tributes of eminent scientists quoted earlier testify in no uncertain manner. I can only conclude that in their enthusiasm they have not sufficiently appreciated the distinction between the logic of science on the one hand, and the practice of research on the other.

It seems to me that professional philosophers suffer from the limitation that they have had no first-hand experience with the subject they are dealing with—practical research in the untidy real world that scientists have to grapple with, full of un-certainties and half-known, ill-defined things. They dwell in the phantom world of symbols and logical abstractions, which, though valuable tools, represent only poorly the medium in which most scientists work most of the time. Seldom do words represent accurately and fully the phenomena to which they apply. Logic deals in words, that is, symbols, not reality.

RESEARCH PROCEDURES

If the philosophers' account of the scientific method is inadequate, then what are the methods characteristic of scientists? Research workers are mostly individualists and independent-minded and consequently there is variety in the ways they tackle problems, for example some proceed systematically while others chase speculative ideas. I do not believe such a thing as *the* scientific method exists, nevertheless there are, of course, procedures that are commonly used in research. The principal ways in which discoveries arise are described in Chapters 1 and 2, and the way their validity is judged is dealt with in Chapter 3. At risk of some repetition, in order to complete the picture I shall outline here a common procedure of a research programme. However, it should not be inferred that investigations always follow such a systematic mode of operation, nor that this includes all procedures used in research.

(a) *Recognition of problem.* The starting point is normally recognition of a problem. This may be an obvious practical problem in, for example, medicine, agriculture or engineering, or it may be a theoretical one arising from dissatisfaction with a prevailing theory. Choosing significant questions and framing them in a meaningful way increases the likelihood of getting informative answers. An endeavour is made to define the problem, to narrow it down to specific components. Semantics may be useful at this stage in helping to clarify one's concepts. It is not always possible—or even desirable—to eliminate all poorly defined words, but at least one should be aware of this possible source of error. Words originally coined for everyday things are often used as terms for little-understood phenomena or mathematical concepts that have no material existence; this practice can be an impediment and a hazard.

(b) *Collection of information.* Relevant information is collected by searching the literature, by systematic observations of the practical aspects of the problem, and enquiries from various sources. Often data need to be classified and perhaps this involves standardization. The data and ideas are recorded and arranged in a systematic way and perhaps tabulated, as recommended by Francis Bacon. One of the difficulties at this stage is to decide what information is relevant; inevitably in selecting material one is influenced by prevailing theories and tentative hypotheses. No-one starts with a clean slate.

(c) *Invention of hypotheses.* This is an activity taking place all the time from the moment the subject is chosen, or even before. This creative part of the investigation has already been discussed in Chapter 1. As many hypotheses as possible are considered and those seeming most likely are selected for testing by experiment or by gathering further observational or survey data.

(d) *Experimentation.* This aspect of the investigation varies so much from one branch of science to another from the technical point of view that it is difficult to generalize. When a hypothesis is very tentative—a mere possibility supported by little or no solid evidence—it is often good tactics first to look for evidence in support of it, either by observation or experiment. When the hypothesis has been developed to the stage where it requires rigid testing, this is done by finding out if it will stand up against experiments planned to produce evidence against it, if possible, a decisive experiment. In biology and medicine usually biostatistics are essential for designing experiments and for assessing results.

In accordance with the precept of Sir Karl Popper and Sir Ronald Fisher, generally the experiment should be designed on the basis of the *null hypothesis*, i.e. a deliberate attempt to falsify the hypothesis being tested. If, for example, the hypothesis is that a particular vaccine prevents a disease, the null hypothesis is that the vaccine has no effect and therefore there will be as many cases in people who have been vaccinated as in those who have not, and the experiment is designed to show this. The null hypothesis is often just the other side of the same coin as the hypothesis, and may not make any difference

Sir Peter Medawar

Sir John Eccles

Sir Hans Krebs

Sir Norman Gregg

to the way in which the experiment is designed, only with the logic of interpreting the results. In the example of the vaccine just mentioned, the question to answer is whether there is or is not a difference between the vaccinated and unvaccinated groups.

Quite apart from the technical and statistical aspects of experimentation, the interpretation of results is not always a simple matter from the logical point of view. Two characteristics, or events, may be shown to be linked, but the relationship may be (i) alternative, (ii) sequential—i.e. a causal chain, or (iii) additive. To give simple illustrations: a broken leg may be multiple causes may be difficult to unravel. Multiple causes may be (a) alternative, (b) sequential—i.e. a causal chain, or (c) additive. To give simple illustrations: a broken leg may be caused by falling down stairs, or by being knocked down by an automobile (alternative); tetanus is caused by a wound that subsequently becomes infected with the tetanus bacillus (sequential, each factor essential); the main causes of atherosclerosis leading to cardiac infarcts are believed to be eating excessive amounts of animal fats, lack of exercise, and smoking; none is essential but the effect of each is additive.

When the results of an experiment are inconsistent with a hypothesis, it is logically proved that the hypothesis is false, provided that the experiment is perfectly constructed and executed, but only then. Even in such a case the hypothesis may still be of value in a modified form. Thus the eventual consequence of an experiment may be rejection, modification or strengthening of the hypothesis; sometimes information may be brought to light that was not anticipated by the hypothesis. Often further experiments are indicated to confirm the results or to clear up some points. The interpretation of experimental results requires the application of many qualities, including logic and creative imagination.

(e) *Publication*. This is an essential part of the research process. Its purpose is not only to share the new knowledge with others, and to claim priority, but also to expose it to criticism. The work must be described in sufficient detail to enable others to repeat it. The findings are interpreted by discussing how they fit into the accepted body of knowledge, and likely implications are suggested. New knowledge is not merely added to the accumulation of old knowledge, it has to be integrated with it. Moreover, as we have seen, it is often publication that leads to further work by others that reveals the true value of the original discovery, for example penicillin.

These are the five principal elements that can be distinguished in a straightforward investigation. I have described them separately for the sake of exposition, but there is seldom a simple progression from (a) to (e). Commonly stages (c) and (d), inventing hypotheses and testing them, go on more or less simultaneously and occupy most of the researcher's time.

There are different mental attitudes appropriate to different stages of the investigation. When carrying out observations, especially in the early stages of the work, the researcher looks for, and pays attention to, the least clue. He plays the role of the detective and follows up the merest hint or suspicion. As John Masefield said with poetic insight: 'from the littlest clue has come whatever worth man ever knew'. This sensitive, explorative attitude of mind is favourable to unanticipated discoveries, as discussed in Chapter 2. The over-sceptical, hard-to-convince scientist is not likely to make discoveries by serendipity. Dr Robert Merton made some pertinent remarks in this connection. '*In general* it's a good thing to know what you are doing—and why you are doing it. The qualifier "in general" is designed, of course, to warn against the danger of that premature fault-finding which stifles ideas that need to be played with before being subjected to systematic and rigorous examination. There is a place, as Max Delbruck and Dickinson Richards have severally reminded us, for "the principle of limited sloppiness".'[72]

During the experimental stage the rigour of logic is applied. Here the researcher must judge the validity of the hypothesis with the searching impartiality of a judge in a law court. It is a mistake to suppose that a clear-cut decision can always be reached. As we have already seen, often hypotheses remain on probation for years. Theories, being generalizations arrived at by induction, can rarely be proved in a formal or dogmatic sense. Almost always they remain open indefinitely to challenge by new evidence, although in practice they are sooner or later either rejected or accepted into the so-called established body of knowledge.

It is often said that one cannot prove a negative. At first sight this appears to conflict with Fisher's rule of the null hypothesis[36] and Popper's principle of falsification. But in fact all three notions are based on the same logical truth, namely, that a *generalization* can not be proved but can be disproved. Most hypotheses are generalizations, and finding many particular instances supporting them never *proves* them to be true in an absolute sense, because it is usually impossible to examine every conceivable instance currently existing, and it is obviously quite impossible to examine future instances, which generalizations normally include as otherwise they are not of much value. On the other hand, a generalization can be disproved by finding instances where it is not true. As Popper said, coherence cannot establish truth, but incoherence and inconsistency do establish falsehood.

Induction has always been recognized by philosophers as difficult to justify as a method of logical inference. Popper and some other modern philosophers reject it; they maintain there is no such thing. But that does not dispose of the problem with which scientists have to contend when trying to interpret data. All the factual information we have to work on concerns past events; we have to generalize from those in order to know what to expect in the future. It is no use ignoring this problem. The philosophical difficulty is partly met by assuming the *principle of the uniformity of nature,* that is, that the characteristics and the behaviour of all things are unaffected by their position in time and space. Such a belief is easy to accept since it is consistent with our everyday experience and all our behaviour is based on it. But the insoluble problem remains, namely, that inductive inference, generalization, intuition, or whatever name you give it, is quite unreliable. Starting from one set of facts, often one can derive several different generalizations, some of which are mutually contradictory, or palpably false in light of other information available to us. We have to fall back on subjective judgement. Much of the anti-pathy to induction seems to arise from regarding it in isolation, as though it were itself the scientific method. It should be regarded as just one of the components of the research process, an essential step toward discovery taken in conjunction with more disciplined forms of thought. It is the spark that starts the fire, which must then be controlled.

In Chapter 3 I have already outlined what actually happens in science: evidence is accumulated until eventually scientists, as individuals and collectively, reach a subjective decision whether or not to accept a particular concept or theory as true, at least for the time being, until or unless contrary evidence is produced. The important thing is to realize that the jump one takes when changing tenses from the past, which describes facts, to the present (implying the future) is based on belief, that is, on subjective interpretation of the evidence. As the Greek philosopher Xenophanes said: 'The final truth . . . is but a woven web of guesses'.

5

Systems theory

'Firstly, there is the unity in things whereby each thing is
at one with itself, consists of itself, and coheres with itself.
Secondly, there is the unity whereby one creature is united
with the others, and all parts of the world constitute one
world.'
MIRANDOLA, 1550

A SCIENTIFIC REVOLUTION

The classical scientific methods that have been used to such
good effect over the last four hundred years concentrate on
the study of factors in isolation. Complex phenomena and
entities are broken down into their constituent parts and the
properties of these examined. This procedure has been described
as the partitionist or reductionist approach. During the last
thirty years it has been realized in many branches of science
and technology that this method fails to take into account
an essential aspect of the world we live in, namely that most
things do not exist in isolation but as integral parts of
organized complexes or systems, and that the elements comprising these systems interact with each other in such a way
that the *whole* takes on characters that are not present in the
separate parts; the unity becomes more than just a simple
collection of the parts. Traditional mechanistic science ignored
this intangible additional 'something' that emerged with
organization, and a basic re-orientation of scientific thinking
was needed to help us understand the essential nature of
systems, organized wholes, meaningful complexity. This has
led to the emergence of a new scientific discipline with far-
reaching theoretical implications and practical applications. It
has been called 'general system theory', 'systems science' or,
more commonly, simply the 'systems approach'.[6, 7, 98] Curiously, the term 'systemology', which has an entry in the

Random House dictionary, does not seem to be used often, although it is apt. The basic concepts are similar to those of the Gestalt theory in psychology, which developed somewhat earlier. Jan Smuts coined the term 'holism' in 1926 to identify a similar idea, but this had little influence on scientific thought as it was put forward principally as a philosophical idea.

The general concept is not a new discovery. It has been recognized by a few writers in philosophy, science, and politics since the classical Greek era, but only during the last thirty or forty years has it received widespread recognition, study, and application. It is no exaggeration to say that systems theory has brought about a scientific revolution in the sense that Thomas Kuhn has defined that phenonemon.[64] This does not imply rejection of traditional methods but the addition of a new dimension to our thinking. Both approaches are necessary.

Systems theory has penetrated into all fields of science, technology, the defence services, industry, and the socio-economic sphere, and has been the subject of innumerable publications and conferences during recent years. This quick growth led to some misapprehensions and inappropriate applications with consequent adverse reactions, but the discipline is now well established. However, not all its ramifications and applications are yet worked out.

One remarkable aspect of systems theory is that, since it has such widespread applications, it provides a unifying theme and a common meeting ground for people working in quite disparate fields of human endeavour. The unifying concept is that of *organization*, which is of universal interest.

The principles of systems theory are easy to grasp, and to use in a general way to gain a better comprehension and to generate ideas in science, technology, and sociology. However, working out the applications in depth commonly involves sophisticated mathematics carried out with the aid of computers.

One definition of a system is 'a set of elements so related that a change in the state of any element induces changes in the state of other elements'.[84] This definition stresses the inter-dependence of the components forming a network but it does not mention an essential characteristic, namely that the whole is greater than the sum of the parts, that something new emerged when the system was set up by nature or by man. Some familiar examples are: the solar system, atoms, man-made machines, telephone networks, airlines; genes, organs, organisms; families, communities, businesses, nations. An automobile is a system, but just a heap of its unassembled components is not. When the components of an aeroplane are properly assembled it becomes a system capable of flying, it acquires a new property not possessed by any of its components alone. A man is a system consisting of a hierarchy of coordinated sub-systems of different levels of complexity— organs, tissues, cells, organelles, macromolecules, etc.

The supreme example of a system having abilities not possessed by its constituents is the human brain, which has some ten thousand million nerve cells, each one having thousands of connections with other cells. The eminent neuro-physiologist Sir John Eccles put it thus:

> The unimaginable organised complexity of the cerebrum has caused the emergence of properties which are of a different kind from anything that has been as yet related to matter with its properties as defined in physics and chemistry. ... Just as in biology there are new emergent properties of matter, so at the extreme level of organised complexity of the cerebral cortex arises a still further emergence, namely the property of being associated with conscious experiences.[31]

All systems, whether physical, biological or socio-political, have certain features in common. The following are their main characteristics.

(a) The components interact harmoniously with one another forming a network of interdependent elements comprising a whole. All the elements are integrated; if there is an element present that does not interact, it is not part of the system. When an organism dies or an automobile is wrecked, they are no longer systems, because their parts no longer interact in a way to ensure the original functions of the system.

(b) A system is more than just the simple sum of its parts. It has a character and properties of its own conferred on it by its organization. A collection of loose parts does not comprise a system, but if, when they are assembled, the whole assumes a new capability, a system is formed. Generally a system has a function or purpose in relation to its environment. One definition of a system is a set of elements interrelated to perform functions or to achieve goals.[37]

(c) If one component is defective, not capable of interacting correctly with the others, not fulfilling its particular function, the whole system is affected. Every part has a role to play. Altering just one element can sometimes have quite unexpected consequences.*

(d) Systems that relate to other systems are called open systems. They depend on other systems for inputs (e.g. food, raw materials) and their output affects other systems (e.g. work, goods, wastes). Virtually all systems are part of ever larger systems (up to the universe) and their components are a series of sub-systems (down to atoms). Closed systems are independent and have no outputs or inputs; in the strict sense there are no such systems, but for purposes of analysis some machines, social groups or organisms are regarded as closed systems.

(e) It follows that systems function in relation to their environment, on which they depend for support and which they affect with their outputs.

(f) Most systems are subject to external constraints imposed by the environment, and internal constraints due to their own inherent limitations.

(g) Many systems, especially in biology, sociology and industry, have a tendency to reach and maintain a dynamic equilibrium (homeostasis). For example our body maintains a constant temperature and fixed levels of blood constituents. These are disturbed occasionally but in-built control mechanisms restore them to within normal limits. Sometimes adaptation may be necessary and involve more or less permanent changes to meet

---

* This idea is of course by no means new. Versions of the following nursery rhyme have been traced back to 1620. During the Second World War it was displayed on the wall in the Anglo-American Supply Headquarters in London.[78]

> For want of a nail a shoe was lost,
> For want of a shoe a horse was lost,
> For want of a horse a rider was lost,
> For want of a rider a battle was lost,
> For want of a battle the kingdom was lost,
> And all for want of a horseshoe nail.

alterations in the environment. The notion of steady state in so-called terminal systems allows for small temporary changes and for larger, gradual, long-term changes. There are also so-called progressive systems that are constantly changing, for example animal embryos, young plants, expanding cities and growing populations.

These seven characteristics are stated here in simple terms so that the general principles can be easily grasped. Some require qualification; for example with reference to (a), in large systems not all components are equally important: some are essential but others can be lost without upsetting the system to any significant extent. With reference to (c), it should be mentioned that some elaborate systems have a built-in potential for self-correction so they continue to function when some component fails.

The application of systems theory to particular cases is generally referred to as *systems analysis*. This term is used in two different senses. It may mean analysing and attempting to explain in words the interrelationships of the constituent elements without quantification or the use of mathematics; a way of thinking about and understanding a system or problem associated with it, concentrating on relationships and the role of each constituent. Alternatively, the term 'systems analysis' is used to describe a group of mathematical methods and techniques for studying quantitatively the various processes and factors involved and perhaps to calculate the effect of altering certain elements. Sometimes it is used to mean much the same as operational research (see Chapter 6), but this is only one use of it.

Systems theory is sometimes confused with *cybernetics*. The definition of cybernetics given by Dr Norbet Wiener who coined the term in 1948 is 'the science of communication and control in the animal and machine'.[99] In the USA the term is now only used to designate the study of information feedback mechanisms, controllers and regulators, especially in engineering, but also in biology and sociology. This is an important part of systems theory but not the whole of it.

The systems approach was first applied as an administrative tool in the military and industrial spheres, and it has become very fashionable in management and engineering. It works best where all the factors can be sharply defined and assigned a value, as in the business world. More recently system techniques have been used in various scientific disciplines and in social studies. However, the problems met in the social field are much more complex than in commerce and consequently the systems approach has been less successful there. There is a risk that it may lead to priority being given to courses of action merely because the factors involved can be defined and valued, to the unfortunate neglect of important alternatives where the elements are difficult to define or put a value on. Commercial and other material considerations could outweigh human values that are subjective and not quantifiable. Is a beautiful view or preservation of wildlife worth more in terms of human happiness than an industrial project that brings employment and material benefits to many?

Systems theory provides a central theme linking a number of modern approaches to the study of complex organizations. These include mathematical modelling, information theory, theory of instructions and programs, games theory, decision theory, catastrophe theory. All these methods may be regarded as comprising the science of studying networks of complexity in which are embedded the problems of the real world. It is now realized that traditional scientific methods, common sense and intuitive thinking are usually quite inadequate for dealing with complex problems. Here linear thinking, in which a causes b, then b causes c with no side effects, fails and may be misleading. Radically new methods are required and a number, such as those just mentioned, have been developed. Most are the products of the marriage of mathematics with science and make use of sophisticated mathematics and computer technology. The basic principles of these methods have been well described in non-mathematical terms in a recently published book by Dr C. H. Waddington aptly entitled *Tools for Thought*.[94] He makes abstract ideas easy to understand by illustrating them with familiar examples. I recommend it to readers who are not mathematically minded but wish to know more about this important and rapidly developing field of study.

REDUCTIONISM

The opposite point of view to systems theory is reductionism, the belief that everything in nature, including living organisms and human behaviour, can ultimately be explained in terms of chemistry and physics. In its crudest form it means that basically there is 'nothing-but' physico-chemical laws, and this thesis has given rise to endless arguments. That the more complex can be explained in concepts appertaining to the simple has been an implicit assumption in science for hundreds of years. Stated simply, reductionism is taking things to pieces to find out what they are made of, and examining the separate pieces; the systems approach is finding out how the pieces interact with each other to enable the whole to function. As a strategy in research, reductionism has been extremely fruitful. There can be no denying that understanding the parts is necessary in order to understand the whole, but it is not sufficient. I doubt if anyone would go so far as to assert that works of art and all the knowledge contained in the *Encyclopaedia Britannica* could be explained entirely in terms of elementary particles.

In 1968 the philosophical questions raised by reductionism were discussed at an interesting symposium organized by Arthur Koestler at Alpbach, a village in the Austrian alps. The fifteen participants were all distinguished in some branch of science. The proceedings, published under the title *Beyond Reductionism. New Perspectives on the Life Sciences*, are wide-ranging, informative and thought-provoking.[61] The main theme is that reductionism, viewed as the philosophy of 'nothing-but' physico-chemical laws, is seriously inadequate as a way of seeking to comprehend nature, since it neglects the special characteristics of organized complexity, especially living organisms. Some speakers consider it virtually synonymous with nihilism. But it was agreed that it is important to distinguish between reductionism as a philosophy on the one hand, and as a strategy in research and basis for planning experiments on the other. Reductionism in the latter sense, that is, analysis into components as a research method, cannot be dispensed with. Arguments on the abstract level about reductionism versus holism or organicism are seen to be pointless when one is engaged in a scientific investigation, for both ways of looking at nature are necessary; they complement each other.

Molecular biology is often cited as an outstanding example of the success of the reductionist attitude. But it has not been pure reductionism. Nobel Laureate Francois Jacob has pointed out that the great advances in this field were made because at every step the analysis of molecules was referred to their function in the living cell.[56] He calls this strategy (simultaneously analysing the simple and the complex and relating them) 'convergence of analysis', and he suggests it will be valuable in studying people and society. Somewhat the same notion has been proposed by Koestler, who developed the concept of a 'holon' that combines the valid aspects of both reductionism and holism. It is at the same time a part and a whole: it is a part of a larger system yet also itself a system with individuality and a degree of autonomy. Like the two-faced Roman god Janus, it looks in both directions at once. Nature consists of a hierarchy of holons.

Jacob's convergence of analysis and Koestler's holon harmonize reductionism and holism, the traditional scientific approach and systems theory.

6

Science as enterprise

'It appears incredible that any such discovery should be
made, and when it has been made, it appears incredible that
it should so long have escaped men's research. All which
affords good reason for the hope that a vast mass of
inventions yet remains.'
FRANCIS BACON, 1620

CLASSIFICATION OF SCIENTIFIC ACTIVITIES

At one time scientific research was mostly conducted by a
few dedicated intellectuals as a sort of hobby. Today it is an
enterprise financed by large funds from government sources,
research foundations, and industry. This necessitates policy
making, planning, and administration. Before discussing these
matters, it will be useful to consider various ways in which
research work has been sub-divided and classified.

Research used to be classified simply as either pure or
applied, with the strong implication that pure research was
concerned with fundamental aspects of science and led to new
knowledge, whereas applied research (or applied science as it
was more often called) was concerned with putting this knowledge to practical use. This distinction has always been easier
to make in physics, chemistry, and engineering than in the
biological and medical sciences. There used to be a certain
amount of intellectual snobbery about pure research, which
was held in higher esteem than applied research. Although
the snobbery has largely disappeared, there still remains much
misunderstanding about the nature of applied research.

In this connection it is interesting to read the eloquent
presidential address to the British Association for the Advancement of Science in 1965 by Sir Cyril Hinshelwood, an
eminent member of the scientific establishment.[50] He had much
to say about the relation of pure and applied science,

especially in non-biological fields. He was at pains to advance the prestige of applied science, yet his words reveal that he still believed at heart that discoveries are made only by scientists and all that inventors do is to apply them. For example in discussing the administration of research, he conceded that it should not be left entirely to creative scientists and dreamers in ivory towers, 'nor is it any advantage to transfer all confidence to the practically minded inventor, who would eventually be left *without any new knowledge to apply*' (the italics are mine).

It is surprising that apparently some people still believe that advances in technology and applied science arise only from discoveries in pure science. This attitude derives from university circles and from the time when practically all worthwhile research was done in universities, which of course is no longer so. The attitude is not justified, because without doubt the solving of practical problems usually requires new ideas and inventive thinking, and sometimes investigation of basic aspects of the problems. Also in the history of science there are many instances of basic principles being discovered in the course of applied research into eminently practical problems. Here are two classical examples. It was while trying to find out whether the king's crown was made of pure gold that Archimedes discovered that the specific gravity of a substance is inversely proportional to the volume of water displaced by a given mass of it. Louis Pasteur laid the foundations of microbiology while investigating the souring of wine, problems with the fermentation of beer, and diseases of silkworms.

One source of misapprehension is the use by Hinshelwood and others of the phrase 'applied science', which interpreted literally can be taken to mean just the application of scientific knowledge in a routine way, as for example when an engineer designs a bridge not involving any novel features. This could more aptly be called the practice of science or technology. But 'applied science' as commonly used means applied research, that is, applying research methods as well as scientific knowledge to the solution of a practical problem. In most contexts the term 'applied research' is to be preferred to 'applied science'.

Nowadays the classification of research has become more

complex as a consequence of public discussions about the deployment of public funds for science. During the controversies in Britain and the USA various notional categories of research have been proposed, but unfortunately this has not always helped to clarify the issues, because the terms used were seldom adequately defined. However, the following categories are now widely recognized:

(a) *Pure research* pursued for the intrinsic intellectual pleasure of exploring and understanding nature and the adventure of discovery, without the deliberate intention of finding something of use. (Nevertheless, discoveries in pure science of course often do have far-reaching practical consequences.)

(b) *Problem-oriented research,* also sometimes referred to as non-targetted or strategic research, may be directed at a particular problem or just at a fairly broad field. One definition is 'that kind of scientific activity considered likely to lead to beneficial results which are nevertheless unpredictable in character'. It is frequently basic research, which has been defined by Drs Comroe and Dripps as research aimed at determining the mechanisms responsible for the observed effects.[16] For example, it would include a study of any aspect of the physiology of reproduction undertaken in the belief that a better understanding of the hormonal and biochemical mechanisms involved may enable one to influence the reproductive process in man or domestic animals in desired ways.

(c) *Goal-oriented,* mission-oriented, targetted or tactical research are synonymous terms describing research planned to achieve a well-defined objective.

(d) *Developmental research* is concerned with the implementation of new knowledge under 'field conditions', adapting techniques where necessary to meet the practical requirements of large scale production and use.

(e) *Operational research* (or operations research) has been defined as 'the application of scientific methods, techniques and tools to problems involving the operations of a system so as to provide those in control of the system with the optimum solutions to the problems'.[30] It is interdisciplinary and commonly is carried out by teams comprised of experts in different fields. It is used mainly in industry and in the defence services and employs the methods of systems analysis. Operational research makes use of scientific and mathematical techniques to investigate the likely effects of adopting various alternative courses of action, thus providing administrators and executives with information that enables them to deploy available resources to the greatest advantage. It helps them decide the best policy, strategy, and action under the prevailing circumstances. This type of research was mainly developed during the Second World War and since has been widely applied in all sorts of industrial and social organizations— railways, supermarkets, coal and electricity supplies, building design, health services, to mention just a few.

These five categories are sometimes useful for administrative purposes, but it should be borne in mind that often the separation is not sharp and one may merge into the other imperceptibly. Any one research programme is likely to make use of several, depending to some extent on the stage of the investigation. Most applied research starts as problem-oriented, goes on to goal-oriented and finally reaches developmental.

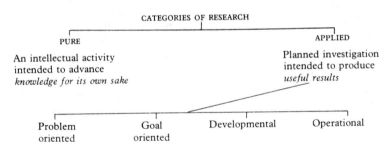

APPLIED RESEARCH

It is mainly the problem-oriented and goal-oriented categories that are relevant to the present discussion (although the developmental and operational categories must also be regarded as particular forms of applied research).

In Britain in 1971 the Government published a report by Lord Rothschild as Head of the Central Policy Review Staff on the organization of government-financed scientific research.[87] At that time the practice was for the Government to allocate funds to the three Research Councils responsible for Agriculture, Medicine, and the Environment respectively and leave the Councils to use the money as they saw fit. Rothschild recommended that about half of these funds should be channelled through the corresponding government departments, which would parcel them out under contract to the Councils for specific investigations which they considered of prime importance from the socio-economic point of view. This was called the customer-contractor principle.

The Rothschild Report caused a furore. The scientific community was almost unanimous in its outcry against the proposals. The Research Councils, the Royal Society and many individual eminent scientists strongly criticized the customer-contractor principle. Dozens of articles were published in *Nature* and elsewhere against the unwisdom of such a way of administering research. 'Only scientists working in a particular field were in a position to decide which direction research should take in that field; to direct them toward defined goals would be a short-sighted policy likely to be sterile; look at the rich rewards, often quite unpredictable, that have come from scientist-generated research under the existing liberal system'— so ran the arguments. Nevertheless, after much public debate and the clearing up of certain misunderstandings, the recommendations were put into effect, but with some compromises.

Similar issues have caused disputes in other countries from time to time. In the USA a study was undertaken by Comroe and Dripps to assess the extent to which some important discoveries in medicine could be attributed to basic or to clinically-oriented research.[16] They found that basic research had played a large part, and concluded that it is pointless to argue which is the more productive as though they were mutually exclusive, and the only question is the proportion of funds that should be allocated to each. They made a plea for much more investigation to be carried out on the nature and origins of scientific discoveries.

An interesting dissertation on the organisation and categorization of government-sponsored research in Britain was given by Professor J. Heslop-Harrison, a distinguished member of the Agricultural Research Council, in his notable 1978 Bewley Memorial Lecture.[49] He described the shock and apprehension caused by the Rothschild proposals, but said that after various adjustments and compromises, the customer-contractor relationship has turned out to be much less objectionable than at first feared. Nevertheless there have been difficulties and some remain. For example, he said that much research cannot be categorized in advance because it is not possible to foresee how deep (i.e. how basic) the investigation will need to go. Heslop-Harrison made a clear distinction between 'applied' research on the one hand and 'basic' or 'fundamental' on the other. He even contrasted 'applied workers' and 'fundamental workers', which seems to me an undesirable and dubious classification.

Another illuminating discussion of the merits of different categories of research was given by Dr B. A. Cross, Director of the Agricultural Research Council's Institute of Animal Physiology, Cambridge, in his 1978 Wilmot Lecture.[19] In a very persuasive address he described some remarkably profitable developments from basic research in animal physiology. He concluded that even 'from the least expected quarter great gains may come', and that the quality of the work is a sounder basis for guidance than is relevance judged in advance. He went on to say 'basic research is not more expensive, more protracted or less productive than applied'.

These two formal addresses by eminent present-day scientists are recent examples of many commentaries on research that have been published, promoting what I believe to be a common and serious misapprehension—confusion about applied and basic research. Like many other critics of Rothschild's proposal, Heslop-Harrison and Cross used the terms 'basic' and 'applied' as though they were opposites and mutually exclusive, reviving in a slightly different form the outmoded views that applied research is just the practical application of discoveries made in pure research. Unfortunately this is a common attitude adopted by scientists, who oppose the direction of research by administrators who see the practical problems that need tackling, instead of just allowing scientists to follow promising lines of investigation. To contrast basic and applied is to confuse classifications using different criteria: one according to the reason the work is undertaken (applied), the other according to the scientific depth (basic). Rothschild himself said applied research is 'indistinguishable from pure in how it is done. The distinction lies in why it is done and who wants it done'.[87] Dr Max Perutz, Nobel Laureate, Director of the Medical Research Council's Molecular Biology Laboratory, said the policy of that Council is to regard basic and applied as inseparable.[80] Some other distinguished scientists have also protested against the separation of research into basic and applied. I think it may be accepted that practically all industrial research is applied, because it is undertaken for commercial reasons—to develop or improve some product or process, or to solve some recognized problem, yet it is sometimes basic. Also I think it is reasonable to consider that since most government-financed research in, say, medicine or agriculture, is sponsored for the useful results it is expected to produce, it is in a sense all applied. The line of demarcation is not always clear, but in principle all research that does not fall within the definition of pure should be classed as applied.

I must admit that my views on categorizing research may be influenced by the fact that I started my research career in Australia investigating disease problems in the hope of eventually finding something that would be of use—problem-oriented, applied research. On the other hand most scientists in Britain started their careers doing pure research in universities and in these circles there used to be—perhaps still is—misgiving about the nature and quality of applied research, which was thought of as all being goal-oriented. Opinions formed early in our life tend to persist. One point on which I am sure all scientists would agree is the need to take a long-term view of research and not to expect quick results, except perhaps in some short-term, goal-oriented projects. Experienced scientists know that most of the time research is frustratingly difficult; the breaks are few and far between. Applied research in the sense I use the phrase is not easier than pure research—indeed it can be argued that it is more difficult, because you have to tackle the problems that are of practical importance, and you are not free to choose the promising ones.

Let us digress for a moment and consider quite a different classification in science, namely, the distinction that is sometimes made between a scientific discovery and a technological invention. Discovery is said to reveal something that already exists in nature (penicillin), whereas invention creates a device or substance that did not previously exist (television, plastics). But those definitions are artificial and in practice the two processes are essentially the same. And in science theories are invented, not discovered, and sometimes in technology new scientific principles are revealed. A more realistic classification of advances in scientific knowledge is: (a) discovery of factual information by observation and experiment; (b) invention of concepts and theories from (a); (c) invention of technical processes and physical things such as machines, gadgets, and new substances.

PLANNING

Planning and management in the scientific field is much the same as in any other enterprise in which there is scope for forward planning on the one hand and personal judgement in operation on the other. A basic requirement is that the actual week-to-week conduct of the investigation—the tactics—be left flexible, but this is not a peculiarity of research planning. Are not flexibility and sensitivity to feedback equally essential to success in business, industry, farming or war?

Discussion of planning research frequently generates controversy, as we have just seen. At one extreme are the advocates of pure science who maintain that research is a creative art and originality does not flourish under direction. At the other extreme are those who assert that research should always be aimed at meeting some need of society, of which there are many crying out for attention. I believe that this dispute is unnecessary and arises mainly because the protagonists on each side, instead of presenting a balanced view, advance only the virtues of their own style of research and misrepresent the other, often tilting at windmills that exist only in their own imagination. In fact, both types of research are essential; they are not mutually exclusive but complementary.

It is helpful to distinguish three levels of planning: *policy* by governments and their advisory bodies, *strategy* by governing councils of institutes and research directors, and *tactics* by the research workers.

At the *policy* level, planning concerns decisions as to what proportion of the available funds should be allocated to particular fields of research, and which subjects within those fields. There are two separate criteria on which judgement must be based: the scientific and the socio-economic. The former assesses the feasibility of proposals, and whether they are likely to produce worthwhile results and advance knowledge. The socio-economic considers the need of society, the cost in relation to likely benefits, and the desirability of the proposals in terms of human values. Value judgements are subjective and must balance anticipated material gains against, say, upsetting our way of life or desecrating the environment. While science itself is objective and free from values, the results it produces affect society, so decision-makers must be sensitive to human values. Therefore at the policy level, scientists, economists, and politically-minded administrators must join in deciding which subjects to sponsor.

Quite apart from the complications of value judgements, it is often difficult to balance agreed needs against scientific considerations. Sir Peter Medawar, in his book *The Art of the Soluble*, explained that scientists have to select problems that in principle appear to be soluble in the current state of knowledge, to undertake only those investigations they think will lead somewhere, and to leave aside for the time being many problems that they know need to be solved but which they cannot see how to come to grips with.[69] For example, it is well known that during influenza pandemics many people become actively infected but do not develop any symptoms. They are protected by some factors we know practically nothing about, referred to generally as non-specific resistance. This is probably more important than immunity in determining who will fall ill and who will not, but so far no-one has been able to see how to investigate non-specific resistance to influenza, so research is concentrated on other aspects of the disease where methods of investigation have been developed. But the 'art-of-the-soluble' principle should not be allowed to dominate all science planning, and some serious problems must be attempted even if at first one cannot see promising approaches. Some problems that initially appeared insoluble have in fact been solved by men with the necessary courage, ability, and persistence. Although there are some things that all would agree are impossible, there are others about which opinions differ; some examples of misjudgement of the 'impossible' have been mentioned in Chapter 3.

An example of the type of problem that I imagine must worry those administering medical research is how to adjudicate between competing demands of funds for research on rheumatism or on molecular biology. The former causes enormous economic losses as well as much suffering, whereas molecular biology does not directly benefit the health of the community. But molecular biology is an exciting and burgeoning field that attracts many scientists and in the long term will have far-reaching effects, while rheumatism is an inherently difficult subject in which progress is slow. Some conservative scientists maintain that the policy of frontal attacks on difficult medical problems like rheumatism is frustrating and fruitless, and the best hope is that developments in some other branch of medical science or biology will incidentally throw light on the problem. This argument tends to overlook the fact that in very many diseases frontal attacks have been highly successful, especially in the infectious diseases. The remaining problems are those in which it has not been successful so far. There is no denying that frontal attacks have in the majority of instances brought great gains, even where they have not completely solved the problem, as for instance in cancer.

In considering planning at the *strategic* level, the foregoing discussion on classification of various categories of research provides a useful background. Broadly speaking, the more that the research is problem-oriented, as distinct from goal-oriented, the more freedom of judgement should be allowed the researcher. And the more freedom of judgement, the higher the quality of the work that should be expected. Mediocre work is not likely to produce worthwhile results at this level, although it may be useful in goal-oriented research which is planned in more detail and so leaves less to the researcher's judgement. Thus planning in problem-oriented research should not attempt to dictate tactics, but only indicate the general lines which it is expected the investigation will follow, always with the understanding that unanticipated findings of significance may necessitate a change of course.

Conversely, the more goal-oriented the research, the more the *tactics* can be projected in advance. Nevertheless, any activity that can properly be called research deals with events and situations that cannot be completely forecast, and therefore some flexibility in tactics should always be allowed to the researcher. Often the type of experiments can be foreseen but the detailed design of each is likely to depend on the results of the previous one.

Defining goals is obviously an important and often difficult task. Decisions should only be reached after full discussions between scientists who understand the more likely possibilities, and administrators and others concerned who know the practical problem and the type of solution that would be desirable. Generally it is inadvisable to attempt to define the goal too precisely. Some of the procedures developed for operational research could be useful here.

Many subjects can be studied at different levels and there may be several partial solutions before the ultimate solution is reached. Let us take a hypothetical example. If the problem is a human disease, investigation may reveal that it is caused by a newly identified bacterium and that the bacterium is susceptible to a certain antibiotic. The disease can be cured: solution No. 1. Later an effective vaccine may be developed and thus the disease can be prevented: solution No. 2. Then study of the ecology of the bacterium may reveal that it has a reservoir in a particular species of animal. Thus people can avoid the disease by taking sanitary measures or avoiding those animals: solution No. 3. Later a method is devised for eradicating the bacterium altogether and the disease disappears: solution No. 4, the ultimate solution. None of the solutions could have been foreseen, except as hypothetical possibilities, and even after they were seen to be scientifically possible, their feasibility and methods for their general application had to be worked out.

The *stage* of the investigation should also be taken into

account in planning research. If the subject is a comparatively new one, or an old one on which little research has been done, the investigation should always be started without any particular goal in mind. All aspects should be investigated in order to get a good comprehension of the whole problem. This might be called exploratory investigation and can be planned at the strategic level. In the early stages full rein should be given to first-hand observation, watching for clues, and imaginative thinking. In the latter stages discovery by serendipity is less likely and there is more scope for rationally planned, systematic experimentation aimed at a particular practical goal.

ADMINISTRATION

Apart from research and development in industry and the defence services, there are four principal ways in which research is administered and financed: (a) research institutes supported directly or indirectly by government funds; (b) universities, and institutes supported by charitable foundations; (c) research initiated and coordinated by international technical organizations; and (d) the grant system.

(a) In institutes financed by government funds the broad programme of applied research is usually determined by a research council, advisory committee or governing body. As we have seen, under the Rothschild policy the relevant government department also plays a part in selecting the problems to be investigated. Generally a considerable degree of discretion is allowed the director of the institute to plan the strategy within the agreed policy.

(b) In universities, and in institutes financed by charity foundations, there is usually a great deal of freedom for the researcher to choose the problem he is to work on, though the head of the department or the director of the institute has of course some say in the matter, if only because he has to provide the necessary facilities and materials. Some of this research is pure, but some is applied because often the researcher and his director have to seek funds from grant-giving bodies, many of which dispense funds of government origin and hence are given mainly for work likely to contribute to knowledge on socially important subjects.

(c) International organizations, such as the World Health Organization (WHO), stimulate research by convening meetings of experts to review current knowledge on particular subjects and to identify aspects where research is feasible and needed for social and economic reasons, such as to combat a disease. WHO promotes research along the recommended lines by inviting selected institutes to undertake the research, and where necessary and possible it helps by providing funds or seeking funds from donor agencies. WHO coordinates research in several countries by arranging meetings of the researchers concerned and facilitating exchange of information in other ways.

Some large research programmes, for example those in human reproduction and in tropical diseases initiated by WHO, are cooperative undertakings supported financially by a wide range of donors including international agencies such as the United Nations Development Programme and the World Bank, national governments, and non-governmental charitable foundations. WHO acts as the secretariat and executive agency and is assisted by an elaborate structure of boards, advisory committees, technical committees, and scientific working groups, which review the field and decide policy, plan the general strategy in particular aspects, coordinate the work world-wide, and keep it under constant review. The implementation of the recommendations of the multifarious activities are instigated and coordinated by WHO. It is able to call on leading experts from its member countries to serve on the various committees. The actual research is carried out in national institutes selected as having the appropriate competency but strengthened where necessary by financial aid and in other ways so that the programme can be pursued in the most effective manner possible.

(d) Under the grant system, researchers at universities or research institutes propose a research project and apply for funds from a grant-giving body, which may be financed from government funds or a charitable foundation. It has become accepted that the successful fund-raiser must devote much time, usually some weeks, to working out his programme. It is commonly known that some researchers are more clever and successful at drafting applications than others; but 'grantmanship' is a poor indication of true merits. There is a strong temptation to exaggerate the importance of the proposed investigation and the likelihood of obtaining valuable results. Applicants who are modest about their expectations and who refrain from committing themselves to a line of action for the following one to three years because they honestly cannot forecast it, are not looked on favourably by administrators and committeemen who sit in judgement. Many scientists have become cynical and say if you want to get the funds you have to play the game according to the rules laid down by those controlling the money.

Requiring detailed programming of a research project, of a series of experiments, is like asking an explorer to charter his proposed course through an unknown wilderness. The planning of each experiment usually depends on the latest results obtained in his own and others' laboratories and even by work in related fields. I believe that the grant system as it has developed inhibits the continued creative thinking of the researcher and his sensitivity to unanticipated clues. It certainly does not encourage serendipity and opportunism. Creative thinking and serendipity, the very sources of discovery, are delicate, sensitive plants that need careful nurturing; they wither all too easily.

The late Professor W. W. C. Topley, one time Secretary of the Agricultural Research Council in Britain, understood research and also committees and was very outspoken in his warning against bureaucracy:

> Committees are dangerous things that need most careful watching. I believe that a research committee can do one useful thing and one only. It can find the workers best fitted to attack a particular problem, bring them together, give them the facilities they need, and leave them to get on with the work. It can review progress from time to time and make adjustments; but if it tries to do more, it will do harm.[93]

No-one would dispute that the allocation of public or charity trust funds must be carefully supervised and it is proper to require the applicant to establish his competency in the field and show that he has a thorough understanding of the particular problem to be investigated. He can also be expected to indicate his proposed general strategy and to show that the necessary basic facilities are available to him. But when it comes to tactics, the able researcher should be given complete freedom —and indeed the obligation and responsibility—to exercise his judgement in light of developments in the course of the work.

Committees are often influenced unduly by members who are good committeemen but may not have a good understanding of research. Also it is curious the way scientists sometimes change their attitudes when appointed to a committee or position of authority; some succumb to the influence of their new environment and adopt the official attitude. But I do not wish to denigrate the importance of administration itself and I am not one of those scientists who look down on all administrators. Obviously efficient management is important in all spheres, for muddled administration can be as harmful as excessive bureaucracy. It goes without saying that the direction of research should be by experienced scientists, but by scientists who combine an understanding of research with an understanding of people and a flair for management. It is not uncommon for a scientist to be a good researcher but inept at handling people and weak on the organizational side of administration.

I doubt if any scientists would disagree with the views I have just expressed. There is nothing new about my criticism of bureaucracy and warning against the harmful effect of overplanning, but it needs to be said again and again in order to keep in check what seems to be a natural tendency for many administrators to expect researchers to proceed in a predetermined, systematic way in an activity where this is inappropriate; they forget that the most worthwhile discoveries are by their very nature unpredictable. I suspect that much of the outcry against Rothschild's proposals arose from scientists' fears of interference by inept bureaucracy rather than from objections to the underlying principle, that part of government-financed science should be aimed at problems recognized by the Ministries as important.

The supervision of research by heads of university departments and directors of research institutes is of course quite a different matter from bureaucracy, and my remarks do not apply there. The successful research director deploys his staff to the best advantage according to their individual talents and experience. He recognizes that the more creative members do best with a minimum of supervision, whereas the less able and less experienced need more guidance. Experienced scientists know that you must feel your way in research. For example, Sir Peter Medawar, former Director of the National Institute for Medical Research, London, said: 'A scientist's reading, discussion with colleagues, and reflections on his latest experimental finding may change the climate of theoretical expectations from *day to day*' (the italics are mine).[71]

It is sometimes said that this is the era of elaborately planned research and team work, and that sophisticated equipment is now a necessity. There is much truth in this view, and it applies especially to certain fields such as nuclear physics. At a recent meeting of the American Physical Society papers were presented with as many as twenty or more authors, and one paper was listed simply as a report of collaboration of three universities and two national laboratories.[51] Nevertheless, it would be quite wrong to conclude that the day of the individual researcher working with modest facilities is over, even in technology. Broadly speaking it is the developmental work that costs big money, whereas expenditure on the research that produces the seminal idea, the initial discovery, is often quite modest. John Jewkes and co-authors give an impressive list of technological developments that sprang from modest beginnings.[57] These include the invention of radio, television, transistors, bakelite, xerography, and the jet engine.

7

Learning the art of research

'Art is simply a right method of doing things'
THOMAS AQUINAS

APTITUDES AND EDUCATION

During the last twenty-five years there has been a boom in research into the psychology of thinking and learning in school children, particularly concerning inventive thinking and ways of fostering it. An important development has been the recognition of two distinctly different types of mind, using different ways of thinking: convergent and divergent. Convergent thinking follows conventional ideas and it uses knowledge that has been taught in order to reach a goal that is accepted without question. It is not the same as critical thinking as defined in Chapter 1, but it has some resemblance to it. Traditional IQ tests measure this type of thinking, and convergent thinkers tend to do well in them and at school examinations provided they have enough basic intelligence.

In contrast, divergent thinkers are more imaginative, they see more possibilities and their answers in tests and in examinations show more originality. They tend to be unconventional in their thinking and are resourceful. They may not achieve high scores in IQ tests. Various tests have been devised to test creative ability and inventiveness, and divergent thinkers perform better in these than do convergent thinkers. It has been claimed that creativity tests measure potential to perform well in the arts and in those professions that put a premium on originality. These tests are often designed to assess three aspects of creativity: fluency (producing many answers), flexibility (a wide variety of answers), and originality (answers different from other people's). A stock question is to suggest many possible uses for a common object; another is to list similarities and differences between two things. But a wide range of tests have been devised and results obtained with different tests do not all correlate well.

Nearly all eminent men and women have an IQ score of at least 120, but beyond that there is no relationship between IQ score and success.[55] A scientist with an IQ score of 130 is as likely to win a Nobel Prize as one with a score of 180. Similarly, performance at university examinations bears little if any relationship to success in science, the legal profession or politics. Two outstanding examples are Darwin and Einstein, who were quite undistinguished at school but revolutionized biology and physics with their theories of evolution and relativity. It is abundantly clear that performance at school and university and at IQ tests are a poor measure of potential for success in science and other walks of life. It has been claimed that creativity tests are a better way of measuring potential, but how reliable and accurate they prove to be remains to be seen. As with IQ tests, there is sometimes a tendency to place more reliance on them than is warranted. It is said by some that creative people often lack application, are poor finishers. This is another characteristic to be taken into account.

One essential characteristic for success that evades quantification is motivation. This is probably determined to a larger extent than the other factors by environmental influences and incentives and by individual interests; therefore the same individual may vary from one subject area to another, and from one time to another.

Having acquired a general framework of scientific knowledge at school, the university undergraduate not only expands his knowledge but also develops a more mature understanding of science. He learns that knowledge is constantly growing and that many currently held theories are provisional, that especially at the frontiers of knowledge there is uncertainty and there are many things still unknown. Convergent thinkers are interested only in what is well established and are indifferent to the rest; the divergent thinkers are intrigued by the

Robert Good

James Watson

Albert Sabin

John Cade

uncertainties and their curiosity is aroused by the unknowns. The former like a feeling of security and order, and may do well in examinations and make proficient engineers, doctors, chemists. The latter enjoy adventure and are likely to be attracted into research or the arts. Convergent thinkers may become competent researchers, and are especially suited to working in a team, under direction, or on a planned, goal-oriented investigation. Divergent thinkers are more likely to become creative researchers working independently or as team leaders. Before the concepts of convergent and divergent thinkers were developed, it was recognized that scientists can be classified as those who work by accumulating information systematically until the conclusion is obvious, as Francis Bacon recommended, and those who are speculative and generate many ideas which they then set about testing out.[8]

It is important to realize that research is not everyone's Mecca, and no-one should embark on a research career unless highly motivated in that direction.

During postgraduate training in research the student seldom receives any formal instruction in the non-technical aspects of research—in the logical and psychological procedures of scientific investigation. The emphasis is on learning by doing rather than on instruction; basically, self-education is what develops one's intellect. The usual procedure in Britain is for the research student to carry out a planned investigation under the supervision of an experienced scientist, and to write a thesis that is submitted to examiners to meet the requirements to acquire a PhD degree. In the USA he is usually also required to take some advanced courses. The most favourable arrangement is one in which the research student becomes virtually an assistant to an active research worker, yet is allowed a degree of independence in working out his own part of the problem. A close master-student relationship is all-important. Sir John Eccles said there is only one way to train people to be creative, that is for them to work with a successful researcher; they should share in the excitement and sense of adventure.[32]

Obviously gaining a PhD degree does not mean that the young scientist knows all there is to learn about the principles and practice of research. For years he will continue to learn from the example and advice of others as well as from his own experience. A few young post-doctoral scientists are fortunate enough to join a research team under the leadership of a distinguished scientist.

THE INVISIBLE INHERITANCE

There have been a few truly great scientists who have had quite a remarkable influence on the young people working with them. In the history of science we find again and again the outstanding scientists have had outstanding teachers.

Sir Hans Krebs, himself a Nobel Laureate, published an essay in *Nature* expounding the theme that good scientists are not so much born as made by those who teach them how to do research.[62] He cited several examples of what he called the genealogy of outstanding scientists. One 'family tree' starting with the great German chemist Liebig last century included more than thirty Nobel Laureates. Another 'family' starting with von Baeyer and extending over four 'generations' included sixteen Nobel Laureates.

Dr Harriet Zuckerman has analysed the background and the university affiliation of American Nobel Laureates.[102] She identified twenty-six laureates, between a third and a half of the total, who were involved in student-master relationships, divided into seven independent 'families'. For example, four of Fermi's students became Laureates, and three of Lawrence's. She pointed out that clusters of Laureates in universities or around an outstanding teacher cannot be attributed entirely to the inspiration and training they receive; they are also partly to be explained on the grounds of selection —the best teachers and universities both attract and select the best young scientists. I would add that there is also the practical point that the apprentice has the advantage that he is working in a new field that has been opened up by the master, so he is in a very favourable situation to gather some of the fruits. There may also be another minor factor, namely, that he enjoys some of the limelight around the great man, so if he does good work it is sure to receive due recognition. Anyone outside the 'establishment', the 'club', has to achieve on his own something quite remarkable to establish his reputation and attract attention.

Dr Michael Polanyi has explained the influence of the master in the following terms:

> In the great schools of research are fostered the most vital premises of scientific discovery. A master's daily labours will reveal these to the intelligent student and impart to him also some of the master's personal intuitions by which his work is guided. The way he chooses problems, selects a technique, reacts to new clues and to unforeseen difficulties, discusses other scientists' work, and keeps speculating all the time about a hundred possibilities which are never to materialize, may transmit a reflection at least of his essential visions. This is why so often great scientists follow great masters as apprentices. Rutherford's work bore the clear imprint of his apprenticeship under J. J. Thomson. And no less than four Nobel Laureates are found in turn among the personal pupils of Rutherford.[81]

Describing the ways in which his master, Warburg, influenced him, Krebs said he set an example of asking the right kind of question, of forging new tools for tackling chosen problems, of being ruthless in self-criticism, of taking pains in verifying facts, of expressing results and ideas clearly and concisely.[63] Krebs also quotes Jacques Monod and Otto Loewi, both Nobel Laureates, talking about what they had gained by working with their leaders. Each spoke of the enthusiasm and excitement of working in a group of highly creative scientists and of the example set by the masters. Above all it is the attitudes of mind and habits of thought rather than knowledge that are imparted by the master to his apprentice. Also the enthusiasm inspired by the teacher brings the habit of hard work, which is looked on as a pleasure rather than a burden.

DEVELOPING A FERTILE MIND

Young scientists who are not fortunate enough to be able to attach themselves to eminent researchers can learn much from reading books that describe the way successful scientists have worked, such as James Watson's *The Double Helix*,[96] Claude Bernard's *An Introduction to the Study of Experimental Medicine*,[4] and T. Martin's *Faraday's Discovery of Electromagnetic Induction*.[68] An important book of this type, of special interest to physicists, was published in 1979: *Einstein: A Centenary Volume*, edited by A. P. French.[38] Also occasional special lectures by eminent scientists, such as presidential addresses and memorial lectures, can be quite inspiring as well as providing a broad outlook on science. An insight into the ways and spirit of great men can be gained from reading biographies such as R. J. Dubos's *Louis Pasteur: Freelance of Science*[29] and M. Marquardt's *Paul Ehrlich*.[67] Some books on the history of science are also appropriate, provided they are written with a real understanding of research and researchers, like Hare's *The Birth of Penicillin*,[47] for example, and are not just a catalogue of events, which unfortunately many are.

By reading the types of books mentioned much can be learnt about how successful scientists went about their work and how they made their discoveries. The important matter to study is not *who* made *what* discoveries, or *when* or *where*, for none of these things will be repeated; they were determined by the course of events now past. What matters is *how* the discoveries were made, for this will be repeated again and again; this, and what led up to them, are the lessons to be learnt.

There should be much more study made of the ways in which discoveries have been achieved. I attempted an analysis in my earlier work, *The Art of Scientific Investigation*, in which are gathered together the experiences and views of many successful scientists.[8] I suggest young scientists will find that book a useful introduction to this fascinating and important subject. There are many aspects of the subject and a lot has been written about it, especially on creative thinking, which, however, is only part of the discovery process. One of the more perceptive articles on the subject that I have read is 'Mainsprings of Scientific Discovery' by Professor Gerald Holton of Harvard University.[51] He speaks of the 'hardly begun study of the nature of scientific discovery'. He points out that creative thinking in science is guided by our basic preconceptions about natural phenomena, for example expecting to find order and symmetry. He calls these beliefs 'thematic presuppositions'.

One of the consequences of the modern developments in cognitive psychology has been the introduction of courses in creativity and problem-solving in a number of American universities.[79] They are based on the premise that to a considerable extent inventiveness is a learned aspect of behaviour. The courses emphasize the importance of imaginative thinking in all walks of life. Obstacles due to perceptual, emotional, and cultural factors are revealed so they can be overcome. For example, cultural and emotional blocks may be due to the habit of conforming, excessive respect for reason and authority, fear of mistakes or failure, or self-satisfaction. An important principle is the separation of the production of ideas from their evaluation. Many of the principles and techniques taught in these courses have already been outlined in Chapter 1. It is said that the courses have a lasting effect on the students' thinking habits, improving their production of original ideas and ability to solve problems.

An important aim of education in any art, including the art of research, is to develop the student's inherent talent, to bring out the individual's particular aptitudes, not just for him to acquire knowledge and learn skills. One way of doing this is to cultivate taste. Taste in the arts is the ability to discriminate between good and bad quality and to appreciate different styles, judgement being subjective and based on aesthetic appreciation. The concept of taste is also applicable to scientific research. One is continually confronted with the need to make a decision on evidence that is insufficient to arrive at a rational conclusion, and action must be determined by personal judgement based on scientific taste. Some scientists refer to this faculty as 'scientific instinct', or 'intuition' or 'feeling'. It has often been said of successful scientists that they were guided by an 'unerring instinct', or that they nearly always guessed correctly. In the arts, taste can be developed by studying assiduously the works of acknowledged masters; similarly in science it can be cultivated by studying the way eminent scientists work. Good scientific taste is only likely to be found in someone who has a real love of science—science as a dynamic world of growing knowledge. The true scientist is delighted and excited when he hears of new discoveries in any field.

However, it would be a sad mistake to take life so seriously and solemnly that there is no place left for a sense of fun. Professor Robert Escarpit believes that effective scientific thinking is helped by an attitude of irreverence towards accepted knowledge, the Establishment, and even oneself, and that the best way of achieving this without becoming irrational is to cultivate a keen sense of humour.[35] A witty joke usually involves a sudden switch in the way of looking at things, an amusing juxtaposition or ridiculous analogy. These are the very thought processes that enable a scientist to escape from conventional views and perceive fresh approaches to a subject. A sense of humour is the best guarantee against becoming intellectually hidebound and having too much respect for the 'conventional wisdom of the dominant group', for which Waddington mischievously coined the acronym COWDUNG. In fact most eminent scientists I know do have a lively sense of humour; they are rarely solemn.

Before ending this discussion of training in research, there is one more point I wish to make. In this book and in my previous one on the subject I have stressed the artistic and creative aspects of science and paid little attention to discipline. This is because the former aspects are the ones that have been neglected in scientific education. Discipline is a basic necessity and I have assumed the young scientist will have received a sound training on this side of the subject. Strictest discipline is required, especially in technical work, in carrying out experiments and observations, and in recording and assessing the results. As Jacques Monod said: 'Research is a game but played with extremely austere and demanding rules; boldness and insight are no use if you don't respect the rules.'[63] A very pertinent remark has also been made by Dr A. H. Coons, who discovered immunofluorescence: 'The educational trick is to teach the habits of discipline without confining the wings of fancy ... the need for disciplined freedom'.[17] Here again the analogy between science and the arts holds good: a poet, composer, or painter achieves success not only through his creative talents, but also because he has mastered a technique through which his creativity can be expressed. There is an old saying that 'he who is the slave to his compass has the freedom of the seas', but one must silently add the proviso 'assuming he has the spirit of creative adventure'.

THE REJUVENATING CYCLE

One of the wonders of nature not sufficiently appreciated is that mankind consists of a succession of generations each of which starts life with brains uncluttered with old knowledge and fixed ideas; fresh slates on which to write new learning. Mature scientists enjoy the advantage of a well-stocked store of knowledge and experience, but they also suffer from the disadvantage that old knowledge often stands in the way of new knowledge and much of their brain's capacity for thinking in new ways has been used up; there are too many well-formed pathways that thoughts flow along automatically. In the young brain the connections between the nerve cells—the memory traces—have not been so often used that thought patterns have become firmly established. Hence randomness of thought has not been lost and the mind is capable of looking at problems in fresh ways. Original ideas come more easily early in life before habits of thought have become ingrained.

In describing how each person's brain has to be trained and patterns of nerve connections established in order to function effectively, Professor J. Z. Young, eminent neuro-anatomist said:

> There seems to be a limit beyond which new patterns and new connections are no longer easily formed. As we grow older the randomness of the brain becomes gradually used up. The brain ceases to be able to profit from experiment, it becomes set in patterns of laws. The well-established laws of a well-trained person may continue to be usefully applied to situations already experienced, though they fail to meet new ones. Here we see with startling clearness the basis of some of the most familiar features of human society: the adventure, subversiveness, inventiveness, and resource of the young; the informed and responsible wisdom of the old.[100]

Generally speaking, great erudition is not the most significant factor in making discoveries. When examined retrospectively most discoveries are seen to have been in themselves fairly simple—especially those involving serendipity. Freshness of mind and the right way of going about an investigation are more important than a vast store of knowledge.

I mention this age factor here to offset any tendency to excessive respect for senior scientists that might inhibit the initiative of young scientists during the springtime of their career. Many pioneering contributions have been made independently by men still in their twenties or early thirties. Hermann von Helmholtz was only 22 when he published a paper indicating that fermentation and putrefaction were vital processes; this provided the starting point for Louis Pasteur's great work. When Albert Einstein was 26 he published three papers that were among the greatest in the history of physics; for one of them he was awarded the Nobel Prize sixteen years later. Long and Morton were both 27 when they began the use of ether as an anaesthetic. Best was 22 and Banting 31 when they discovered insulin. James Watson was 25 when he and Francis Crick worked out the double helix structure of DNA. Richard Shope discovered the influenza virus when he was 29. Robert Wilson was 28 and Arno Penzias was 31 when they discovered background radiation. Ignaz Semmelweiss was 29 when he recognized that puerperal fever was an infectious condition. Van Grafe devised the operation for cleft palate and founded modern plastic surgery when he was 29. Claude Bernard had started his famous research on the glycogenic function of the liver when he was 30.

According to Dr H. C. Lehman, who made a study of the subject, the most productive decade of life for scientists is most commonly between 30 and 40.[65] The average age at which American Nobel Laureates carried out their prizewinning work was 39, although they did not receive the award till twelve or thirteen years later.[103]

For making discoveries, 'the adventure, subversiveness, inventiveness, and resource of the young' are much more important than 'the informed and responsible wisdom of the old', to borrow J. Z. Young's words.

8

The brave new world

'O brave new world, that has such people in it'
SHAKESPEARE

MEN WHO CHANGE THE WORLD

For building a cathedral many skilled craftsmen are needed,
but only a few architects; similarly for building the edifice of
science many competent scientists are needed, but only a few
highly creative individuals. In science the distinction between
the various workers is not really so clear-cut, but the analogy
drives home the point that there are different types of scientist
and it is necessary that it should be so. The scientists one reads
about are nearly all exceptional men, leaders in their field, and
they are not typical of the scientific community as a whole. They
are the architects and it is interesting and instructive to learn
about them, but it would be a mistake to suppose that all
scientists are similar or that they ought to be.

In most respects scientists in general are as varied in their
character traits as are any other professional or business group;
they are just a cross section of any community they belong to.
But the exceptionally productive scientists—the pioneers who
open up new fields—have certain features in common that are
not seen in the same degree or so frequently in other people.
I believe there are five traits that are characteristic of these men.

First I would put intellectual curiosity, which all outstanding
scientists possess to a marked degree. They want to understand
what lies behind the phenomena they observe, what are the
underlying reasons for things being the way they are; they have
a sense of adventure in trying to find things out, a thirst to

explore the unknown. Their curiosity is linked with the creative impulse, for the desire to know is not only to satisfy their own inquisitiveness but also to fulfil their urge to produce something original of their very own—a theory or a solution to a practical problem.

Second, they are tremendous enthusiasts. They frankly enjoy their work and get excited when the work goes well. This makes them inspiring leaders of teams and teachers, for enthusiasm is contagious. When someone is emotionally committed to a task, his moods are likely to vary according to how the work is going, therefore it is not unusual for scientists to have periods of great activity and excitement alternating with periods of depression when the work is frustrating. Occasionally this mood-fluctuation may come close to manic-depressive behaviour. In fact, I had two friends who were frankly manic-depressives; they were brilliant researchers but died at the height of their careers.

Third is a strongly developed independence of mind. The leaders rely on their own judgement of the evidence and are not much influenced by other people's. They may be frank to the point of self assertiveness and they have a habit of scepticism. Sometimes this characteristic may give the impression of intellectual arrogance, for it shows a lack of respect for the views of others. It may be manifested in the form of dogged persistence in the face of seemingly insuperable obstacles, discouraging advice from colleagues, or adverse criticism. Dr Albert Sabin said 'No matter how good you are, you cannot be a scientist unless you learn to live with frustration.'[88] He said a good scientist is likely to achieve one gratification for every hundred frustrations, and the mediocre scientist will have to labour through a thousand. Innovation often requires daring, even some rebelliousness. When scientists have suffered from severe opposition, abuse and even persecution, their courage has been sustained by faith in their own convictions. The real innovator is sometimes an isolated person, a 'loner'.

Fourth, a liking and capacity for working hard and for exceptionally long hours, often to the extent that little time is left for family life and recreation. Some of the leading scientists in America today are said commonly to work 120 hours a week.[85] By choice they are truly dedicated to their work, which comes before all else. As with many great artists and explorers they are possessed by a tremendous driving force that has nothing to do with motivation for personal material gains.

Fifth, they are ambitious in the sense of desiring fame, and of striving to achieve and to get credit for their successes. Great importance is attached to establishing priority of publication for a discovery and for getting due recognition of that priority. Esteem from fellow scientists is highly prized. They feel intensely about their work and often overvalue their ideas and hold an exaggerated estimation of the importance of their work. A few, by no means all, and perhaps not the greatest, have the temperament of the proverbial prima donna; they jealously guard their claim to their creation, their bit of immortality.

One could list many other character traits, such as a desire to benefit mankind, to make the world a better place, competitiveness, a good intellect and a lively imagination, but these qualities are seen often also in leaders in non-scientific spheres. A musical talent is rather frequently shown by scientists; probably it is related to the artistic and creative side of science.

The 'human' characteristics of some of the most famous medical researchers in America have been portrayed in a book written by a journalist, Donald Robinson, called *The Miracle Finders*.[85] Robinson interviewed some dozens of eminent scientists and he describes their personalities and their views on their work and achievements. I know personally several of those about whom he has written and can confirm that he has painted a fair picture of them. However, I think he has exaggerated the jealousy and antagonism that undoubtedly does exist to some extent between certain of those he depicts. I believe a generous, helpful attitude prevails more often than meanness and denigration of rivals; it certainly does in Britain and Australia and I believe also in the USA. In these matters scientists are probably no worse than other sections of the community; I like to think that, if anything, they are rather better; at least that has been my experience.

REACTION TO SCIENCE AND TECHNOLOGY

In Chapter 3 I referred briefly to the adverse reaction against science and technology by many non-scientists. This is a serious matter that requires further consideration. The most extreme form of this counter-culture was the hippie movement, which has now largely subsided. But dissatisfaction with the effects of science and technology on society is more widespread and it has given rise to serious attempts to reconsider their proper role in our civilization.

The main undesirable features of modern civilization for which science and technology are blamed are the following: (a) the Bomb and other highly destructive war weapons, (b) harmful or unpleasant side-effects of many technological developments and products, especially various forms of pollution and degradation of the environment, (c) mass production techniques that have destroyed the satisfaction of work and displaced creative crafts, (d) excessive urbanization and crowding associated with industrialization, (e) frequent displacement of people to seek work and consequent disruption of family life, and (f) the dehumanizing effect of the computer in administration. Also there is apprehension about coming developments such as widespread use of nuclear energy, genetic engineering, techniques for controlling human behaviour, test-tube babies, and various fanciful possibilities portrayed in science fiction. Too rapid changes in life style have disrupted traditional customs and caused instability and thus feelings of insecurity and unhappiness. Greater efficiency in technology has led to unemployment. It is said by the critics that science and technology have no regard for human values and that they erode the cultural and spiritual side of life, reducing man to a mere puppet. Scientists are accused of arrogance, irresponsibility, and disregard for people's feelings. Some of the more extreme critics deplore the dominance of reason and objective thought because they undermine religious beliefs and therefore ethical systems based on them. They assert the superiority of feeling, poetic intuition, and even mysticism.

This is a formidable list of charges. Let me say straightaway that scientists in general are just as concerned as others about many of them, especially the Bomb. The Bomb is a dreadful abuse of science for which political leaders and others in power are at least as much, if not more, to blame as are the scientists involved. Most of the other undesirable features of modern life can be regarded as side-effects that are only indirectly attributable to science and technology. They are the consequences of industrialization. Science and technology are responsible only in that they have placed enormous power in the hands of industrialists, politicians, and society generally. The unpleasant side-effects are the price society has had to pay for the benefits gained. But most of these are not inevitable and scientists are striving to minimize them insofar as it is in their power. However, the problems are often difficult. For example, there are an estimated 63,000 chemicals being used commercially in the USA and something like 1,000 new ones are being added annually. Testing this number of substances for various types of possible ill-effects is not only a formidably large task, but the methods available are imperfect, especially regarding long-term effects. Chemicals contribute significantly to living standards; controlling them involves substantial economic consequences. The Environmental Protection Agency is charged with the difficult task of making regulations based on technical methods that often have an element of uncertainty.[95]

Material side-effects, such as pollution in its various forms, can usually be countered by putting into effect various technical remedies, but this is largely a matter of economics and politics. Controls need to be enforced and paid for, and ultimately the cost falls on the public. The sociological and psychological problems are more complex. Change in living conditions is usually painful, even when it is for the better, and time is needed to readjust to the new circumstances and establish new patterns of living. It is said by many, and with some justification, that technocracy, and scientists individually, commonly undervalue the importance of non-intellectual human experience. Human values, intuitive feelings, taste, and emotions should not be neglected to the extent they often are by scientists. Therefore it would benefit everybody if the education of scientists included more studies in the humanities than it ordinarily does in most universities. It has been said that narrow specialization produces 'learned ignoramuses'; they are learned in one field and grossly ignorant in the humanities and even in other branches of science. Such people are unable to understand or appreciate the political, social, and moral questions thrown up by science.

The late Professor Jacques Monod, author of the classic *Chance and Necessity*, believed that the present day discontent is due to science having undermined traditional mythical beliefs and religions that provided a basis for ethical behaviour and value systems.[74,75] He said that this is probably the greatest revolution that has ever occurred in human culture and it is at the very root of most present day social discontent. Since the dawn of civilization man has longed to find an explanation of the mysteries surrounding him, and to meet this need he developed religious beliefs. These provided a foundation for tribal unity and ethical behaviour that had survival value. Consequently this mental trait of faith in myths has probably become ingrained in our genetic heritage. The big question is whether science can offer an alternative that people can embrace. Monod believed that the solution lies in an ethical system based on objective knowledge and reason, something that I think most scientists adhere to in principle, but this creed has not yet penetrated into society as a whole. In this 'ethics of knowledge' the object to be revered—the foundation—is knowledge for its own sake. This could provide the framework of a new scientific humanism.

Writing in similar vein, Dr Francois Jacob, the molecular biologist who shared the Nobel Prize with Monod in 1965, pointed out that traditionally all cultures provided their members with a unified and coherent view of the world and the forces behind it.[56] Religions based on myths offered comprehensive systems that explained everything and this gave a feeling of security to the believers. In contrast, science confronts belief with the actual at every step, the theory with the experiment. Its picture of the world is incomplete and often uncertain, it does not pretend to encompass everything. It is a different way of thinking, a different outlook on life, to which mankind needs to adjust. I suggest that we need to bear in mind that man is a newcomer in the world compared to most other members of the animal kingdom. *Homo sapiens* is a very young species and is still in the process of adaptation.

A point made by Professor W. H. Thorpe at the Alpbach Symposium was that much of the public criticism of science today is due to the misconception of science as reductionist and mechanistic in terms of outdated ideas of physics that were deterministic and left no place for free will.[61] Physics itself is no longer purely materialistic and there are no grounds in modern science for denying human values.

Dr Paul Couderc believes that the anti-science trend arises from ignorance of the true nature of science on the part of most non-scientists.[18] They do not understand its methods, its concepts, its capabilities or its promise. It is essential for the future of a healthy society that a basic understanding of science, its principles and practice, not so much the technical information, be made part of the cultural equipment of everyone. This would enable people to adjust mentally to the new world and also make them more receptive to future technological advances. Couderc says the need is for more sound and widespread popularization of science, and scientists have a responsibility to society to do this. It is a duty especially appropriate for senior or retired scientists. A keen sense of communication is essential in order to capture the audience. Scientists who lack this facility may profitably collaborate with a professional writer.

It surprises me that so little has been said in defence of science and technology. There can be no doubt that the benefits far, far outweigh the undesirable side-effects and will continue to do so, provided only that a nuclear war is not started by the politicians. The average person in the industrialized countries today has more freedom from disease, malnutrition, discomforts, and ignorance, and more amenities than were enjoyed even by the few very rich and powerful a century or two ago. The quality of life in western civilization has improved beyond all measure. People are no longer obliged to labour twelve to fourteen hours a day for six or seven days a week; they now have leisure time and the wherewithal to indulge in cultural activities, sport, and other recreations. I doubt if historians, who know what life was really like in the mythical 'good old days', are among those who deplore modern civilization.

SOCIAL RESPONSIBILITY OF SCIENTISTS

There has been much debate for a number of years about how far scientists should be responsible to society for the results of their work. This question applies particularly to university scientists as they are the ones who are free to choose their field of research. The greater number of scientists today work for government sponsored bodies, or in industry; in their case the responsibility lies mainly with the authorities that employ them; they are not entirely free agents, short of resigning from their post.

In 1979 legal charges were brought against the University of California claiming that agricultural research which it promoted had led to increased automation and consequently farm workers losing their jobs. The University's defence was that the results of the research have been of benefit to the community as a whole through increased productivity and lower food prices, and that in any case the social consequences of its research were the responsibility of the whole community rather than of the University.[26]

In 1970 the British Society for Social Responsibility in Science held an international conference in London on 'The Social Impact of Modern Biology'. Twenty eminent scientists, including three Nobel Laureates and six Fellows of the Royal Society, presented papers which were subsequently published along with the discussions in a book edited by Dr Watson Fuller.[39] It was generally accepted that within the next few decades developments in the biological sciences will radically change civilization as we know it today. Discoveries used wisely can be of immense benefit to mankind, but many can also be used in ways that either intentionally or unintentionally have disastrous effects on man and on the other inhabitants of this planet. Most scientists feel involved and have well-developed consciences in these matters, but the problems are extremely complex. In the first place scientists—especially those doing pure research—often do not know what sort of discovery they are likely to make, or, having made it, they cannot foresee the eventual impact on society. Very occasionally a scientist may find himself in a cruel dilemma.

The conference indicated that most scientists do have a feeling of responsibility toward society, but how far they are able to influence the applications of their work is another matter. What they can do is to keep the public informed and especially to advise politicians and other influential persons. When a new technical development becomes available it should be examined by a commission on which all sections of the community are represented, including of course scientists competent in the particular field. The universities have a role to play here in that they can provide unbiased experts. The scientists should make the technological assessment of foreseeable benefits and adverse effects, and these should be clearly stated for all to see, but the decisions and responsibilities should be shared by all sections of the community. One of the problems is to arrive at a consensus about social values and goals. Public debate through the media is essential in helping to shape values and make choices, but everyday experience of politics in democratic countries shows how difficult this often is.

One of the clearest statements I have read about the social responsibilities of scientists is an article by Nobel Laureate Sir Ernst Chain.[15] First he makes the point, with which I agree, that the general run of scientists outside their own specialty are no wiser than non-scientists, nor are they free from prejudice and emotional attitudes. Indeed even within their own field they are sometimes intolerant of the views of colleagues with whom they disagree. Their advice should be sought and respected on technical, factual matters within their competence, but outside that most scientists should be regarded in the same light as other citizens of comparable standing. Chain concludes that scientists cannot be held responsible for the obnoxious effects of their inventions; responsibility lies with the society that adopts the technological application. It is up to society to take—and pay for—measures against the unwanted side-effects such as pollution or invasion of privacy. Like others, Chain says that one thing scientists can and should do is to counteract the tendency of the news media to exaggerate and sensationalize new developments.

A point on which all scientists agree as an ideal when discussing these matters is that a scientist should be responsible for presenting a true picture to the public about new developments in his own field, and for indicating possible implications so far as he can see them. But of course scientists working in the defence services are rarely free to do this, nor are most of those in industry. A final word: whatever critics may say or wish, today science is an extremely important part of our culture, and modern civilization is in fact based on technology; there is no going back, and science and technology will influence our lives and the world we live in to an increasing extent. Therefore man will have to adjust to this situation as he has to other changes. Scientists must take a positive part, individually and collectively, in helping people understand the spirit of the brave new world. Jacques Monod has made an important contribution with his exposition on scientific humanism in *Chance and Necessity*: 'the transcendent kingdom of ideas, of knowledge, and of creation—a kingdom that is within man'. These aspirations are consistent with the views that Albert Einstein expounded in *The Religious Spirit of Science*.[38]

SHAPING THE FUTURE

The growth of science and technology over the last hundred years has completely changed our way of life, both physically and culturally. Last century no-one could have imagined the changes that science would bring. And the speed of growth of knowledge is accelerating. As the 'known' expands, so does contact with the 'unknown' and therefore the scope for yet more rapid extension. Knowledge breeds new knowledge. The progression is geometric. Thus there is good reason to believe that the next hundred years will bring still greater technical developments and still more understanding of nature—including 'human nature'—than the century just past. But what about the next 1,000 years, 10,000 years, 100,000 years, million years? We just cannot see so far, it is out of the reach of our imagination.

There are some scientists and non-scientists who believe that there are certain areas of knowledge that should be regarded as forbidden fruit—nuclear energy and genetic engineering, for example. But whatever the prophets of doom may say, man will inevitably explore these and as yet undreamt-of hazardous areas with consequences we cannot even guess at. It is entirely possible that an unimaginable catastrophe such as a nuclear war will befall mankind, but personally I take an optimistic view and believe the future is more likely to bring heaven on earth rather than hell. If the already existing technology were universally applied, it could bring a physical paradise; but there is a grave lag in the social sciences and it will take some centuries even at a continuously accelerating rate of progress before universal happiness prevails. By this I do not mean some simplistic notion of a paradise where people are just amusing themselves all the time, but rather freedom from undue physical and mental discomforts, plus contentment through pursuing absorbing interests; and variety would be an essential feature.

It is evident that man has become so powerful, owing to advances in science and technology, that he really is shaping the future—both his own and that of all the other creatures with which he shares this planet. The forces at man's command are now too powerful, and the consequences too difficult to foresee, for it to be sufficient to rely on common sense, unaided reasoning, or just to let things take their course and see what happens. No powerful action can be expected to have only one consequence. As we have learnt from systems theory and associated disciplines, any disturbance of one part of a system can have unexpected and far-reaching effects.

Throughout the whole of evolution there has been a rough balance of species. Some disappeared but new ones emerged and the marvellous variety we see today was preserved. If one species multiplied excessively it would be reduced by disease, famine or other checks. But man has virtually escaped from the constraints of nature and has already gone a long way toward changing the biosphere, suiting his ends to the detriment of many of our fellow creatures. The laws of biology have been overridden. If present trends continue, only about one per cent of the Earth's surface will remain in its natural state by the turn of the century—only twenty years hence—and a large proportion of the animal species will be doomed to extinction.[28] Political and religious leaders should realize that the greatest crime—sin—mankind could commit, against not only our fellow creatures but also against future generations of man, would be to allow the human species to multiply to the extent that it usurped the whole biosphere and squeezed out most other species. Mankind would be condemned to live forever in the dullest of worlds, a concrete jungle shared with a few species that thrive under those conditions—such as cockroaches and rats.

Whether one is an optimist or a pessimist about the consequences, it is clear that science has placed a tool in the hands of one species of the animal kingdom that bestows potential far beyond that inherent in his natural design.

There are heartening signs that public concern has at last been aroused about such fundamental matters affecting the future as the population explosion, conservation of nature, pollution of the environment, and exhaustion of natural resources. But already it is late—later than most people realize. Initial attempts are being made to study the world as a gigantic system—a complex of complexes: the Total Problem or World Problematique. There is an urgent necessity to develop tools for thought, to borrow Waddington's metaphor, in order better to comprehend the world we live in and foresee the consequences of our actions and be warned of disastrous trends before it is too late.[94] It may be necessary to forego the advantages of short-term expediencies, such as consuming non-renewable resources, or despoiling the environment, if in the long term the effects are ruinous. That is a preliminary need. Then comes the enormously difficult problem of persuading mankind to act collectively to avoid disaster. Men of goodwill must not be deterred by pessimists and believers in determinism, who say that man cannot shape his own destiny, because he is carried along in the inexorable stream of evolution, which includes social behaviour and is beyond his control. Many eminent philosophers and neurophysiologists believe, and I do, that man does have free will in many spheres of thought and action. The fact is that man *is* making decisions and taking actions that determine the future; let us strive to make wise decisions based on the best forecasts that can be made with modern methods of operational research. The fact must be faced that man now *is* shaping the future and he must shoulder the responsibility for planning it.

Having discovered tools and learnt to develop them vastly, we need to find within ourselves, and to cultivate, the wisdom to handle them for the good of future generations of man and of our fellow creatures. This should not be beyond our capacity, considering that we have at our disposal the intellectual, practical, and moral faculties that have taken us out of the caves and wildernesses of our origin. Surely it is high time for responsible people to stop dreaming wishfully of personal immortality in the 'next world'. We need a crusade to save *this world* and make it a heaven and not a hell for our children's children's children. . . .

Afterthoughts

'There are more things in heaven and earth than are dreamt
of in your philosophy.'
SHAKESPEARE

Before ending this book I would like to indulge in some
philosophical reflections.

The world may be regarded as consisting of material objects
and immaterial phenomena or processes (for want of a better
term for theories, information, organization, and abstractions
generally), hardware and software, to borrow the expressive
jargon terms from computer technology. The humanities and
arts have always been concerned mainly with software, while
the sciences have dealt mainly with hardware, although they
have used the software of ideas and theories to handle the
material things. At one time, some scientists took the view that
only material things were 'real' and that concepts and theories
were abstractions that existed only in people's minds, but now
nearly everyone realizes the shortcomings of this narrowly
materialistic view of the world.

Organisms, including you and me, are made up of common
raw materials that are of no significance in themselves; only
when organized into a meaningful pattern, a dynamic system,
do they constitute a living entity with characteristics and
capabilities that are not possessed by the raw materials. It is the
organization, that immaterial ingredient, that makes us what we
are, not the material components. There is a turnover of the
actual constituents, but the pattern remains essentially the
same for a considerable time. The whole, the Gestalt, is very
much more than just the sum of the parts.

What is the nature of this immaterial ingredient? At one

time some thinkers tried to explain it by postulating a vague concept called the 'vital force', but vitalism implied a mysterious supernatural agency that was incomprehensible and unacceptable to most scientists, so the idea has long since been rejected in favour of a more mechanistic view of living things. Last century and the first half of this, most scientists believed that, in principle, all biological phenomena could be explained ultimately in terms of physics and chemistry. This reductionist, mechanistic philosophy was based on the assumption that if we could find out enough about the components we could explain the whole. Modern scientific thought, under the influence of systems theory, recognizes the need to take into account an extra ingredient, that cannot be weighed or measured and eludes detection by instruments, because it is intangible, abstract, neither matter nor energy. It is difficult to conceptualize or define. The nearest I can get to it is 'a pattern that conveys both information and a program of instructions', which I shall refer to simply as 'Pattern' for short.

As we have seen in Chapter 4, we encounter the same conceptual problem, not only in living things, but also in any complex system, whether naturally occurring or man-made. And the same applies to man's artistic creations. If we consider music and literature, for example, we can see the same phenomenon in a form in which the Pattern is not tied to particular material constituents and therefore is a little easier to see as having an independent existence. Here the Pattern is capable of existing as an entity made of different materials and yet retaining its character. A musical composition can be stored and transmitted by notation on sheet music, on a gramophone disc, on magnetic tape, in the human brain, or can take the form of a pattern of sound produced by an instrument or orchestra. Much the same applies to a Shakespearian play which, in addition, can be translated into various languages and the phantom characters still live and play their parts as they did in the author's mind three hundred and fifty years ago. The Pattern is clearly very much more important than, and just as real as, the material constituents—paper and ink. The former has a degree of immortality, and a life of its own, that the latter has not.

Like the creations of great writers and musicians, the Pattern that built you and me is also immaterial and immortal. It is written in the genetic code relayed down in the DNA of a succession of germ cells from generation to generation for thousands of years. The same Pattern made the Pharoahs and earlier men, with only relatively minor variations. Incidentally, it is remarkable that all genetic information acquired by living organisms throughout evolution is written in the same 'language'—the DNA language, which has an alphabet of only four chemical 'letters', arranged in a double helix.

The scientist's business is creation of human knowledge, which in itself is immaterial (and immortal), though commonly it is about material things. There is an analogy between constructing a physical system composed of parts plus organization and synthesizing a theory by putting together data and ideas in a new meaningful way; in both cases something that did not exist before is created.

Many scientists today are acutely aware that there are important aspects of nature not encompassed by science; it is not so much lack of knowledge as the limitations of the traditional scientific outlook. Koestler ably reviewed the situation in 1978 in his book *Janus. A Summing Up*.[60] He said it is high time that all scientists escaped from ingrained habits of thought that were appropriate for nineteenth-century materialistic science—reductionism, determinism, and causality—but are no longer tenable as universal truths in light of present day physics. Those adhering inflexibly to such restrictive dogmas are like the people living in H. G. Wells's *Country of the Blind*, denying the reality of many bizarre phenomena because they are beyond their comprehension. A fundamental shift of outlook on the part of scientists might bring a harmonizing relationship of science and valid aspects of mysticism, might open the frontier between objective knowledge and subjective awareness. The great mystics, religious visionaries, and artists experience deeply internal insights that cannot be described adequately in language, but are nonetheless real. Truth as the scientist conceives it must be capable of being demonstrated objectively and made explicit so others can fully comprehend it. Nevertheless many aspects of creativity are shared by all great thinkers when grappling with elusive problems of the abstract world. Einstein said: 'The most beautiful emotion we can experience is the mystical. It is the sower of all true art and science.'

Abstract ideas and symbols are tools that mathematicians and theoretical physicists are accustomed to using, but many scientists—at least biologists of my generation—do not feel secure with them unless they can be related directly to material things and we can form a mental model made of familiar things. Many of us regard with suspicion concepts concerned with intangibles and verging on the metaphysical and mystical. In Chapter 2 we saw that even mathematicians dealing with astrophysics hardly believed their symbols represented real events. Perhaps the younger generation of scientists brought up with a different background may be better equipped mentally to handle these concepts and yet still exercise the rigour of disciplined scientific thought. I hope that my amateur philosophizing may encourage them to extend their horizons beyond the practicalities of the laboratory bench, while still respecting the basic principles of scientific integrity.

Appendix

Archimedes' discovery of the principle that the specific gravity of a material is inversely proportionate to the volume of water it displaces was described by the Roman architect Vitruvius, who lived about the beginning of the Christian era. This account was written some two hundred years after the discovery, so it may not be true in every particular. However, Archimedes' own writings contain some evidence in support of it. The following paragraphs are from a translation by Professor Frank Granger of Nottingham.[44]

Archimedes made many and various wonderful discoveries. Of all these the one which I will explain seems to be worked out with infinite skill. Hiero was greatly exalted in the regal power at Syracuse, and after his victories he determined to set up in a certain temple a crown vowed to the immortal gods. He let out the execution as far as the craftsman's wages were concerned, and weighed the gold out to the contractor to an exact amount. At the appointed time the man presented the work finely wrought for the king's acceptance, and appeared to have furnished the weight of the crown to scale.

However, information was laid that gold had been withdrawn, and that the same amount of silver had been added in the making of the crown. Hiero was indignant that he had been made light of, and failing to find a method by which he might detect the theft, asked Archimedes to undertake the investigation. While Archimedes was considering the matter, he happened to go to the baths. When he went down into the bathing pool he observed that the amount of water which flowed outside the pool was equal to the amount of his body that was immersed. Since this fact indicated the method of explaining the case, he did not linger, but moved with delight he leapt out of the pool, and going home naked, cried aloud that he had found exactly what he was seeking. For as he ran he shouted in Greek: eureka, eureka.

Then, following up his discovery, he is said to have taken two masses of the same weight as the crown, one of gold and the other of silver. When he had done this, he filled a large vessel to the brim with water, into which he dropped the mass of silver. The amount of this when let down into the water corresponded to the overflow of water. So he removed the metal and filled in by measure the amount by which the water was diminished, so that it was level with the brim as before. In this way he discovered what weight of silver corresponded to a given measure of water.

After this experiment he then dropped a mass of gold in like manner into the full vessel and removed it. Again he added water by measure, and discovered that there was not so much water; and this corresponded to the lessened quantity [volume] of the same weight of gold compared with the same weight of silver. He then let down the crown itself into the vase after filling the vase with water, and found that more water flowed into the space left by the crown than into the space left by a mass of gold of the same weight. And so from the fact that there was more water in the case of the crown than in the mass of gold, he calculated and detected the mixture of the silver with the gold, and the fraud of the contractor.

References

1 Ashby, Eric (1971). 'Science and antiscience', *Nature (London)*, **230**, 283.
2 Austin, J. H. (1978). *Chase, Chance and Creativity. The Lucky Art of Novelty*. Columbia University Press, New York.
3 Bacon, Francis (1620). *Novum Organum*.
4 Bernard, Claude (1865). *An Introduction to the Study of Experimental Medicine*. English translation. Macmillan, New York, 1927.
5 Bernstein, Jeremy (1979). *Experiencing Science*. Burnett Books, London.
6 Bertalanffy, L. von (1968). *General System Theory*. Braziller, New York.
7 Bertalanffy, L. von (1969). 'Chance or law', in *Beyond Reductionism*, Ed. A. Koestler and J. R. Smythies. Hutchinson, London.
8 Beveridge, W. I. B. (1957). *The Art of Scientific Investigation*, 3rd edition. Heinemann, London; Norton, New York.
9 Beveridge, W. I. B. (1972). *Frontiers in Comparative Medicine*. University of Minnesota Press.
10 Beveridge, W. I. B. (1977). *Influenza. The Last Great Plague*. Heinemann, London; Prodist, New York.
11 Bodmer, Walter (1978). 'A man of great influence', *New Scientist*, **80**, 702.
12 Buck, Carol (1975). 'Popper's philosophy for Epidemiologists', *International Journal of Epidemiology*, **4**, 159.
13 Burnet, F. M. (1972). 'Immunology as a scholarly discipline', *Perspectives in Biology and Medicine*, **16**, 1.
14 Cade, John F. C. (1949). 'Lithium salts in the treatment of psychotic excitement', *Medical Journal of Australia*, **36**, 349.
15 Chain, Ernst (1970). 'Social responsibility and the scientist', *New Scientist*, **48**, 166.
16 Comroe, J. H. and Dripps, R. D. (1976). Scientific basis for the support of medical research', *Science (New York)*, **192**, 105.
17 Coons, A. H. (1961). 'The beginnings of immunofluorescence', *Journal of Immunology*, **87**, 499.
18 Couderc, Paul (1971). 'An Antidote for anti-science', *Impact of Science on Society*, **21**, 173.

19 Cross, B. A. (1978). 'Discovery and application. Lessons from animal research', *Veterinary Record*, **102**, 548.
20 Culliton, B. J. (1974). 'The Sloan-Kettering affair', *Science (New York)*, **184**, 644 and 1154.
21 Dawson, E. B., Fieve, R. and Sheard, M. L. (1974). 'Shall we put lithium in the drinking water?', *Proceedings of the Seventh International Water Quality Symposium*, Washington, p. 47.
22 Dawson, E. B., Moore, T. D. and McGanity, W. J. (1972). 'Relationship of lithium metabolism to mental hospital admission and homicide', *Diseases of the Nervous System*, **33**, 546.
23 de Bono, Edward (1969). *The Mechanism of Mind*. Cape, London.
24 de Bono, Edward (1970). *Lateral Thinking: A Textbook of Creativity*. Penguin, London.
25 Delp, P., Thesen, A., Motiwalla, J. and Seshadri, N. (1977). *Systems Tools for Project Planning*. International Development Institute, Indiana University.
26 Dickson, David (1979). 'University challenged over "Agribusiness" connections', *Nature (London)*, **278**, 768.
27 Dorfman, D. D. (1978). 'The Cyril Burt question: new findings', *Science (New York)*, **201**, 1177.
28 Douglas, John (1978). 'Biologists urge U.S. endowment for conservation', *Nature (London)*, **275**, 82.
29 Dubos, R. J. (1950). *Louis Pasteur: Freelance of Science*. Little, Brown & Co., Boston.
30 Duckworth, W. E. (1962). *A Guide to Operational Research*. Methuen, London.
31 Eccles, John C. (1970). *Facing Reality. Philosophical Adventures by a Brain Scientist*. Springer-Verlag, New York. Permission to quote kindly granted by the publishers.
32 Eccles, John C. (1975), in Krebs and Shelley, *loc. cit.*
33 Edwards, M. J. Personal communication.
34 Edwards, M. J. (1978). 'Congenital defects due to hyperthermia', in *Advances in Veterinary Science and Comparative Medicine*, **22**, 29. Academic Press, London.
35 Escarpit, Robert (1969). 'Humorous attitude and scientific inventivity', *Impact of Science on Society*, **19**, 253.
36 Fisher, Ronald A. (1935). *The Design of Experiments*. Oliver & Boyd, London.
37 Flagle, C. D. (1972). *Systems Analysis Applied to Health Services*. Pan American Health Organization, Washington.
38 French, A. P. (1979). Editor, *Einstein: A Centenary Volume*. Heinemann, London.
39 Fuller, Watson (1971). *The Social Impact of Modern Biology*. Routledge & Kegan Paul, London.
40 Garfield, Eugene (1977). 'Negative science and the outlook for the flying machine', *Current Contents*, **20** (No. 26), 5.
41 Glick, B., Chang, T. S. and Jaap, R. G. (1956). 'The bursa of Fabricius and antibody formation', *Poultry Science*, **35**, 224.
42 Gordon, W. J. J. (1961). *Synectics. The Development of Creative Capacity*. Harper & Row, New York and London.

43   Gould, Stephen J. (1979). 'Smith Woodward's folly', *New Scientist*, **82**, 42.

44   Granger, Frank (1934). *Vitruvius on Architecture Vol. II*. Permission to quote kindly granted by The Loeb Classical Library (Harvard University Press: William Heinemann Ltd., London).

45   Gregg, N. M. Personal communication.

46   Halstead, L. B. (1978). 'New light on the Piltdown hoax?', *Nature (London)*, **276**, 11.

47   Hare, Ronald (1970). *The Birth of Penicillin*. Allen & Unwin, London.

48   Harvey, Bill (1978). 'Cranks and others', *New Scientist*, **77**, 739.

49   Heslop-Harrison, J. (1978). 'Research, crop production and policy', *Annual Report Glasshouse Research Institute* 1977 (Supplement).

50   Hinshelwood, Cyril (1965). 'Science and scientists', *Nature (London)*, **207**, 1055.

51   Holton, G. (1975). 'Mainsprings of scientific discovery', in *The Nature of Scientific Discovery*, editor O. Gingerich, Smithsonian Institution Press, Washington.

52   Holton, Gerald (1979). 'What, precisely, is thinking? Einstein's answer', in *Einstein: A Centenary Volume*, ed. A. P. French. Heinemann, London.

53   Hope, A. (1976). 'Raw deal for inventors?', *New Scientist*, **71**, 430.

54   Hope, A. (1979). 'The battles of Armstrong—radio's forgotten man', *New Scientist*, **81**, 306.

55   Hudson, L. (1966). 'The question of Creativity', in *Creativity. Selected Readings*, ed. P. E. Vernon (1970). Penguin, London, p. 231.

56   Jacob, François (1977). 'Evolution and tinkering', *Science (New York)*, **196**, 1161.

57   Jewkes, J., Sawers, D. and Stillerman, R. (1958). *The Sources of Invention*. Macmillan, London.

58   Koestler, Arthur (1964). *The Act of Creation*. Hutchinson, London.

59   Koestler, Arthur (1971). *The Case of the Midwife Toad*. Hutchinson, London.

60   Koestler, Arthur (1978). *Janus. A summing up*. Hutchinson, London.

61   Koestler, Arthur and Smythies, J. R. (1969). Eds. *Beyond Reductionism. New Perspectives on the Life Sciences*. The Alpbach Symposium 1968. Hutchinson, London.

62   Krebs, Hans (1967). 'The making of a scientist', *Nature (London)*, **215**, 1244.

63   Krebs, Hans A. and Shelley, J. H. (1975). Eds. *The Creative Process in Science and Medicine*. Proceedings of the C. H. Boehringer Sohn Symposium, Kronberg. Excerpta Medica, Amsterdam; American Elsevier Publishing Co., New York.

64   Kuhn, Thomas S. (1970). *The Structure of Scientific Revolutions*. University of Chicago Press.

65   Lehman, H. C. (1943). 'Man's most creative years: then and now', *Science (New York)*, **98**, 393.

66   Magee, Bryan (1973). *Popper*. Fontana, London.

67   Marquardt, M. (1949). *Paul Ehrlich*. Heinemann, London.

68 Martin, T. (1949). *Faraday's Discovery of Electromagnetic Induction.* Arnold, London.
69 Medawar, Peter B. (1967). *The Art of the Soluble.* Methuen, London.
70 Medawar, Peter B. (1975). 'The scientific method in science and medicine', *Perspectives in Biology and Medicine*, **18**, 345.
71 Medawar, Peter B. (1978). 'March of paradigms', *Nature (London)*, **273**, 575.
72 Merton, Robert K. (1975). 'Thermatic analysis in science: Holton's concept', *Science (New York)*, **188**, No. 4186, 335. Copyright 1975 by American Association for the Advancement of Science. Permission to quote kindly granted by the author and publisher.
73 Miller, P., Smith, D. W. and Shepard, J. H. (1978). 'Maternal hyperthermia as a possible cause of anencephally', *Lancet*, **1**, 519.
74 Monod, Jacques (1971). *Chance and Necessity.* English translation. Knopf, New York; Collins, London.
75 Monod, Jacques (1971). 'On the logical relationship between knowledge and values', in *The Social Impact of Modern Biology*, ed. W. Fuller. Routledge & Kegan Paul, London.
76 Nicolle, Charles (1932). *Biologie de l'Invention.* Alcan, Paris.
77 Nossal, G. J. V. (1975). *Medical Science and Human Goals.* Arnold, Melbourne.
78 Opie, Iona and Peter (1951). *Oxford Dictionary of Nursery Rhymes.* Oxford University Press, London.
79 Parnas, S. J. (1963). 'Education and creativity', in *Creativity, Selected Readings*, ed. P. E. Vernon (1970). Penguin, London, p. 341.
80 Perutz, Max F. (1972). 'Health and the Medical Research Council', *Nature (London)*, **235**, 192.
81 Polanyi, Michael (1946). *Science, Faith and Society*, Riddell Memorial Lecture. Oxford University Press. Permission to quote kindly granted by the publishers.
82 Popper, Karl R. (1972). *Logic of Scientific Discovery.* Hutchinson, London. Permission to quote kindly granted by the publishers.
83 Rescher, Nicholas (1978). *Scientific Progress. A Philosophical Essay on the Economics of Research in Natural Science.* Blackwell, Oxford.
84 Roberts, Richard (1978). 'From modest beginnings', *Nature (London)*, **275**, 689.
85 Robinson, Donald (1976). *The Miracle Finders. The Stories behind the most important Breakthroughs in Modern Medicine.* McKay, New York.
86 Rosenfeld, L. (1967). In *Niels Bohr. His Life and Work as seen by his Friends and Colleagues*, ed. S. Rozental. John Wiley, New York.
87 Rothschild (1971). 'Two views of British science', *Nature (London)*, **234**, 169; **234**, 313.
88 Sabin, Albert (1973). 'I only asked for a place to work', *New Scientist*, **57**, 490.
89 Schaefer, M. (1974). *Administration of Environmental Health Programs. A Systems View.* Public Health Papers, No. 59, World Health Organization, Geneva.
90 St. James-Roberts, Ian (1976). 'Cheating in Science', *New Scientist*, **72**, 466.

91   Stoker, Michael (1976). 'Fact, fiction and fraud', review of *The Patchwork Mouse* by Joseph Hixson, (1976). Anchor/Doubleday, New York. *Nature (London)*, **264**, 126.

92   Taton, R. (1957). *Reason and Chance in Scientific Discovery*. Trans. by A. J. Pomerans. Philosophical Library, Hutchinson, London.

93   Topley, W. W. C. (1940). *Authority, Observation and Experiment in Medicine*. Linacre Lecture. Cambridge University Press.

94   Waddington, C. H. (1977). *Tools for Thought*. Cape, London.

95   Walsh, John (1978). 'EPA and Toxic Substances Law: dealing with uncertainty', *Science (New York)*, **202**, 598.

96   Watson, James (1968). *The Double Helix*. Athenaeum, New York.

97   Weinberg, S. (1977). *The First Three Minutes. A Modern View of the Origin of the Universe*. Deutsch, London.

98   Weiss, Paul A. (1969). 'The living systems: determinism stratified', in *Beyond Reductionism*, ed. A. Koestler and J. R. Smythies. Hutchinson, London.

99   Wiener, N. (1948). *Cybernetics*. Wiley, New York.

100 Young, J. Z. (1951). *Doubt and Certainty in Science. A Biologist's Reflections on the Brain*. Clarendon Press, Oxford. Permission to quote kindly granted by the publishers.

101 Young, J. Z. (1978). *Programs of the Brain*. Oxford University Press.

102 Zuckerman, Harriet (1967). 'The sociology of Nobel prizes', *Scientific American*, **217**, 25.

103 Zuckerman, Harriet (1977). *Scientific Elite. Nobel Laureates of the U.S.* Macmillan, New York.

104 Zwicky, Fritz (1969). *Discovery, Invention, Research Through the Morphological Approach*. Macmillan, Toronto.

Index

D₃

D